HOW GOOD ARE YOUR VIRTUES?

HOW GOOD ARE YOUR VIRTUES?

The Transforming Power of Love

LANCE WEBB

ABINGDON PRESS   Nashville

DEDICATED TO

ELIZABETH
JEANNE, MARY, AND RUTH

My wife and daughters
in whose dear companionship I have discovered
some of the deeper meanings of divine giving-love
that makes all life beautiful and worthwhile.

MY THANKS
to Mrs. Agnes Campbell and Mrs. Virginia Wilcox
for their help with the manuscript.

HOW GOOD ARE YOUR VIRTUES?
The Transforming Power of Love

A Festival Book
Copyright © 1959 by Abingdon Press

Festival edition published May 1983

ISBN 0-687-17528-3

Printed in the United States of America

CONTENTS

PREFACE

To the Second Edition

"Hell is the home of honor, duty, justice, and the rest of the Seven Deadly Virtues. All the wickedness on earth is done in their names. Where else but in hell should they have their reward?"

This book is not about hell, though these words from George Bernard Shaw's Don Juan in *Man & Superman* describe very well the hell of useless suffering even in this life when we neglect or refuse the wondrous giving-love of God, enabling us to discover and give love to ourselves and others.

After writing my first book, *Conquering the Seven Deadly Sins* (now being reprinted with the title, *How Bad Are Your Sins?*), I was asked by a young attorney member of my church, "Do you mean that pride is always a sin?" I answered, "No, there is a healthy pride. We ought to be proud of our heritage, of our opportunities and blessings." This led me to realize that the opposite of the sin of pride is the virtue of humility, and that humility itself may be vicious and hurtful. So I wrote this book, intending to use the title, *Love Conquering the Seven Deadly Virtues*. However, the title *Discovering Love* was chosen as simpler and less disturbing to many readers who might not understand how a virtue could be deadly! Looking back over these years, I am very sure that all of us need to be disturbed by what sometimes is called "Christian love" that is neither Christian nor virtuous. Hence the title chosen, *How Good Are Your Virtues?*

Humankind is threatened by self-destruction not only by nuclear bombs and electronic war, but also by the self-hatred and self-righteous conflict and alienation in broken lives and homes. Above all else we need to discover and accept the real love that means the beginning of heaven even on earth.

How could a virtue be deadly? The answer of the Bible and other records of human experiences is that no matter how seemingly good

7

our virtues are when they are unaccompanied by Divine Giving-Love, they are vicious indeed.

This book is intended to describe that precious love and to show how in everyday living its presence in our attitudes and acts makes the difference in our heaven and hell and for those around us in the world now while we live! Each chapter deals with one of the classical "virtues" and shows how without this gracious love transforming it, each one becomes indeed a deadly vice!

Again, I express my thanks to Abingdon Press for sharing my vision of two companion volumes both of them bearing the subtitle, "The Transforming Power of Love." I hope that any and every reader who needs disturbing will be disturbed and that all who read may be encouraged and enabled to accept the noble gift of loving and being loved.

Lance Webb

I. When Love Is Real

We all hunger for love. More eagerly than a blind man seeking for light, a drowning man for air, or a starving man for food; more ardently than a Christopher Columbus looking for a new route to the East; more yearningly than a homesick boy dreaming of home, we hunger and thirst for love—that sweet mystery of life that turns darkness into light and keeps the light from going out, that turns evil into good and keeps the good from spoiling.

There is one supreme good in human life—the ability to love and be loved. To be "in the kingdom of heaven" is "to love God supremely and your neighbor sincerely"! Thus said the man whose own life is the highest revelation of love known to mankind. And true neighbor-love includes not only those of another nation or class or race but—and often this is much more difficult—your wife or husband, your father and mother, your son and daughter, your own brothers and sisters, who by their acts are sometimes your enemies.

> I never knew an hour so drear
> Love could not fill it full of cheer! [1]

"Hearts unlovely and unloved," on the other hand, is the deadly evil from which all other evils come. "Hell is not to love any more," says Georges Bernanos. It is to be "capsuled in ice" says Dante in his *Inferno*, as he pictures the lowest regions of the damned. *Love or Perish* is the title of a well-known doctor's latest book. We know this to be true, even those of us who are unable to find love although we may desire it with all our hearts. [2]

[1] John Kendrick Banks, "I Never Knew a Night So Black."
[2] Smiley Blanton, *Love or Perish* (New York: Simon & Schuster, 1956).

One of the most difficult enigmas of human life is this matter of love. We talk about it, write about it, sing about it, cry over it, extol it to the skies, and bewail it to the depths.

"Water Can't Quench the Fire of Love!" So runs the popular song. Some of us are not quite sure. At least, if water can't quench the fire of love, there are other things that can, such as hate and selfishness, folly and fear!

There are many who have been betrayed by love—or what masquerades under the name of love. Two young people fall in love and marry, perfectly sure they will love each other "till death us do part." But sometimes in a matter of weeks they discover they now can't stand each other. "If we love each other," they complain, "why do we fight and hate each other so?" *Why do we so often hurt those we love most?*

A parent, speaking of a wayward child, asks, "What's the matter with my love? I loved him with all my heart and did everything I could to help him. I gave him everything—see all the things I did for him. How could he treat me so?"

On the other hand, there are those like Paul who are perfectly sure that love never fails!

> Love is patient and kind. . . .
> Love bears all things,
>   believes all things,
>   hopes all things,
>   endures all things.
> Love never ends.

They, like Robert Bridges, know from experience that "love is a fire in whose devouring flames all earthly ills are consumed." They agree with Julian Huxley, the biologist, that "love is a positive emotion, an enlargement of life; it leads on toward greater fulfillment and counteracts human hate and destructive impulses. . . . Love is indispensable!" [3]

[3] "All About Love," in *Look*, July 12, 1955.

Clearly there is a wide chasm between the failing, disappointing, despairing kind of love displayed by tens of thousands of young couples and fathers and mothers, and the love pictured by Paul, and Robert Bridges. What a difference between love that hurts and devours, and love that "heals, cultivates, protects, and inspires." [4] All that which we call "love" is *not* good, does *not* heal, cultivate, protect, and decidedly does *not* inspire! There is a kind of "love" that is devilish and evil.

There is also a love which never fails, because it results in the fullest growth and maturation of personality for both the loved and the loving. This is the answer to our deepest longing. This is the love we seek to discover.

The Inadequacy of Words

Immediately we come up sharply against the inadequacy of our human speech to convey the meaning we would like to impart. Any definition of so precious an experience as that represented by the word "love" leaves us cold. How can you put into words that which is contained in our deep, inner, spiritual experiences? Someone has compared this difficulty to that of describing in two sentences a whole year's adventures in a foreign land. You can give the facts but the real experience can only be hinted at. And yet if we are to communicate with any degree of helpfulness in considering the enigma of love, we will have to use words and to put into them as much meaning as possible.

Surely the English word "love" is woefully inadequate for the load it is expected to bear. We call upon it to express all kinds of different meanings: love of God for man; devotion of man to God; love between man and woman; loyalty to country; love for a dog or a watermelon; possessive love and affirmative love; strong love and soft, weak love.

[4] Blanton, *op. cit.*, p. 2.

11

It is obvious, therefore, if we are to continue using the English word "love" we will also need to use some descriptive adjective with it or else we cannot be understood. Hence, the title of this chapter, "When Love Is *Real*." *Real* or *genuine* love we shall use to designate the love which never fails, which is "the end of all our living." The other kind of destructive, hurtful love is real too in the sense that it exists, but not in the sense that it is the answer to our deepest needs and longings. It is a counterfeit of the real love for which we are meant.

Love is an attitude and not purely a feeling, an idea, or even a passion. It is the response we give to others. If it is real, the response is healthy and creative. If it is false or twisted, the response is unhealthy and negative.

The Greek language does better by having different words for different kinds of love. The apostle Paul and other New Testament writers used the Greek word "agape" to differentiate between the two kinds of love. "Let love be genuine," cries Paul:

Put on then, as God's chosen ones, holy and beloved, compassion, kindness . . . and patience, forbearing one another and, if one has a complaint against another, forgiving each other; as the Lord has forgiven you, so you also must forgive. And above all these put on love [agape], which binds everything together in perfect harmony. (Col. 3: 12-13.)

That is, agape love toward another person is like God's love toward us: a creative, unconditioned acceptance of us even with all our sins and failures; and an outgoing response of the Divine Concern with compassion and forgiveness "which binds everything together in perfect harmony."

Real love is responding to others in the same way God responds to us. How does God respond to us? Our Hebrew-Christian faith declares that God relates himself to us with gifts of blessings un-

12

numbered. Our whole lives are made possible by this generous, self-giving love of the Eternal. As Christians we go further to declare that the greatest, most amazing gift of God's agape love is the gift of his Son, Jesus Christ: "God so loved the world that he gave his only Son, that whoever believes in him should not perish but have eternal life" (John 3:16). This Divine Agape is given to us not because we are worthy by our good deeds, our perfect morals, or by any intrinsic goodness we may possess, but because we are his "chosen ones" created for his fellowship and for love ourselves.

The real love for which we are intended, therefore, is first of all a wholehearted response to the love of God in adoration, in thanksgiving, and in trusting acceptance of ourselves as loved by God and therefore precious in his sight. As a result of our acceptance of the love of God, we are then able to love others in a creative, helpful way. This then is the contribution of Christian faith to our deepest need for real love: We are to love others as God loves us, and when we do, our love always brings out the finest of our own capacities and helps to do the same for others.

False or inadequate love, on the other hand, is the failure or refusal to relate to others with this spontaneous, unconditioned outgoing response. It may be represented by a second Greek word, "eros," which means the response we make to those who are lovable and deserve our love. Eros love is a possessive, conditioned, acquisitive response that desires relationships with the other person primarily for what he or she already is or may be able to do for us. In Chap. III these two loves are differentiated as "giving-love" and "desiring-love." It is not appropriate to take any more space in this introductory chapter to describe them, except to say that giving love to others as God gives love to us is the real love we seek. Desiring-love, seeking to find in others that which is desirable and lovable to us, is inadequate love. All of us possess desiring-love at times, and certainly it is not to be dispensed with in our human experiences or to be condemned; yet unless our love goes beyond

13

desiring, to learn the creative joys of giving-love, we will find increasing frustration instead of the joyous goal of living.

A Definition in Life

The best place to begin our quest for real love is in the very place where most of us are with our first great difficulty. This difficulty is not primarily a matter of words or definitions but of attitude. It resides in two facts: (1) we are more interested in being loved than in loving; and (2) we do not know how to love.

The first basic problem is accepting myself as loved in the sight of God; as belonging in a universe where I am not an orphan, unloved and unimportant, but where I am precious and valuable, with infinitely greater possibilities than I have ever imagined or dreamed. This problem will be dealt with primarily in the second chapter but will be considered in its appropriate relationships in the other chapters.

The second basic problem is how to love others with this wise giving-love as God has loved us. This will be the major concern of the remaining six chapters.

Through all that follows it must be remembered that love is a mystery, one of the deepest and most profound of all mysteries. It cannot be captured in a word or a phrase or even in a poem or a book. It can only be lived. It comes from those deeps of the soul where we are most akin to the deeps in the universe and can, therefore, come only to him who has faith to go beyond things seen and felt.

A young man who thought he had a scientific mind, while reading one of John Keats' love sonnets, said impatiently, "I can never understand why people rave so about love. It is nothing but a simple biological process." [5] Such a person will find life vulgar and common. He will cheat himself out of the most real, the most lasting and priceless experiences of life. He will lose the chief glory

[5] *Wisdom* Magazine, April, 1957, p. 48.

and victory in life, the one clue to the meaning of suffering and death, and the victory of the human spirit over it.

It is to be hoped that, though this book cannot present you with love itself, it may, even through the use of words, help you to discover what the old Romans believed even before they had heard of Jesus, "Amor omnia vincit"—love *does* conquer all!

II. Discovering Myself as Loved

Grace N., an attractive young Irish woman of twenty-five, confessed that though she earnestly longed to be loved she was unable to love any one man for very long. Instead, she became bored with each of them in turn. Writing to Mary Haworth, who conducts a counseling column in several daily newspapers, she said this of her many romances:

I'm afraid to admit to myself that I am a bad girl. . . . When I first arrived here I started dating and having a gay time, and met lots of boys and had many romances, but . . . just drifted from one to another. . . . What does a girl do?—G. N.

Mary Haworth's answer is a classic in the diagnosis of love's difficulties:

Dear G. N., Love isn't necessarily a grand and glorious blaze of delight, shared by two. Essentially, love is a "set of the will"—a deeply organized purpose to devote oneself to the furtherance of another's good. . . . You haven't known love as yet, because inwardly you are too hostile against mankind, and too self-despising.

This lovely little Irish woman was not a bad girl in her intentions toward others, but primarily in her intentions toward herself. Her trouble was that she could not truly love herself; in fact, she hated herself though she would have been the last one to admit it, because from her earliest days she had felt that the self she knew had betrayed her and let her down.

No doubt, rejection on the part of parents or playmates or friends was partly responsible; but back of this rejection by some of the persons and groups to whom Grace was related was the deeper sense of being orphaned and unwanted in the world. She felt lonely, like a child lost in the woods of an Immense Indifference. She was continually being threatened in these bleak woods by the wolves of insecurity, with their companions of anxiety, jealousy, and hate. She wanted to believe in herself, to love herself, and spent all her energies trying to prove herself to herself. But with all her attempts she was unable to love anyone deeply and generously. She was not oversexed, as she thought. She was underloved.

While Grace's experience may not correspond to our own either in detail or degree, it does indicate one of our deepest problems as human beings in a vast universe which seems to take great pains to emphasize our littleness and unworthiness. And when our inadequacies are underlined by the continual rejection of some of the unloving people around us, it is no wonder that we begin to doubt ourselves and unconsciously even to hate ourselves for being so inadequate and so unlovable.

Or to put it in a different way, our deepest need is to discover how to free our powers to endure, to create, to love, and to live up to the real measure of our possibilities. To think greatly of ourselves and our powers is not wrong, as some have misunderstood it to be. It becomes the deadly sin of pride only when we fail or refuse to evaluate ourselves by the love of God, the name the Hebrew-Christian faith gives to the deepest Reality at the heart of all things. Rejecting this evaluation of our *true* selves, we center our attention too much on our *false* selves. Our compulsive efforts to prove ourselves in false ways lead us to dejection and frustration, because we can never pile up enough evidence to satisfy our insatiable craving for evidence of our adequacy and of the worthiness of our love. Our sin of pride is the attempt to pose as God, pretending to be able to manufacture heaven with its love and peace and creative achievement. We need above everything else to discover who we are and to accept ourselves as we are in deed and in truth.

Who Am I?

Most of us, according to the opinion of many psychologists, use only one twentieth of our potential. All of us, with but few exceptions, will confess that we spend too large a part of our energy in fighting the negative emotions of fear, resentment, frustration, and inadequacy. Why? Because we are lacking in the courageous humility that declares with thankful confidence: "What I am in God's sight, that I am, no more and no less."

But what am I in God's sight? What is the truth about myself and my relations to Ultimate Reality? The answer to this basic question determines my ability to love and to accept myself as loved —the ability to be free and creative, at my best. Obviously, this takes me into the realm of faith. There is no other way. We have to choose our faith, and we live by the faith we choose.

Are we orphans in a meaningless universe, left to fend for ourselves and to decide whether or not we are going to love others and seek to promote their well-being?

Are there no values except of our own making? If not, then the question of accepting myself and loving myself becomes extremely difficult. For I do not want to be an animal. I do not want to die, to lose my identity in nothingness. I do not want to be an orphan, to be rejected by the universe even as I am rejected by so many of my fellows. Therefore, I hate myself for being nothing but a speck of dust in the gleam of a million, million suns. I long for infinitely more than this. I think there must be a God—some great Intelligence who has made me for himself so that I am restless until I rest in him, as Augustine put it. I want to belong in my universe, to believe that my intelligence, my will, my power to love and to give myself sacrificially for others, is but a reflection of the Infinite Intelligence, the Almighty Will, the Eternal Love that is at the heart of all things. I need to believe that I am valued by this Intelligent Love, not because of what I am but because of the nature of what God is. In that secure relationship of Eternal Love, I would be able to see things in their true perspective, to accept myself and to begin living the loving, creative life I was meant to live. To this experience tens of thousands in every age have testified. Those who have believed it are the ones I admire the most —Schweitzer, Grenfell, Father Damien, and Jesus Christ himself.

I have to choose my faith: either I will accept and live by the love of God or I will not. How do I decide which faith to choose? The best and surest way is to regard the evidence in the lives of those who have accepted it and in those who haven't. This chapter is intended to point to this clear and unmistakable evidence in the life of mankind. Wherever and whenever man has committed himself to live by his faith in the love of God, he has been able to accept himself and to love others. This is not true, obviously, of the millions who nominally profess to believe in the love of God, but only of those who have *living* faith:

> An affirmation and an act that bids Eternal Truth
> be present fact!

First, look at what happens when I lack this kind of basic self-acceptance in the love of God. Then my anxious ego, filled with rigid pride, attempts to reach four foolish and impossible goals:

1. To prove my superiority, since I feel so inferior.
2. To prove I am adequate, for I feel so inadequate.
3. To prove my failure is not my own fault, and thereby make my cowardice seem courageous.
4. To prove I am not guilty when I feel so guilty.

These four goals are unattainable because they are contrary to Reality or God. That God is love is evidenced by the creative results of my self-acceptance, which I may discover as countless others have done before me.

I. Love Needs No Proof of Superiority

Being unwilling to accept my real self as loved and lovable in the sight of Eternal Love, I may use even humility and unselfishness as a shield from the real self I am unwilling to accept, and as a proof of my superiority to others. The humility and unselfishness may really be my own self-despising and self-loathing, caused by my inability to prove myself superior as my inner compulsions demand, rather than the courageous humility and the loving unselfishness which belong to those in the kingdom of heaven.

Of course, if one is proud of his humility and is self-centered in using his unselfishness to make everyone admire and praise his virtue, then he is neither humble nor unselfish. This is exactly the point: he *thinks* that he is humble and unselfish, and therefore that he has no sin of pride or selfishness to consider and to overcome. His virtues are smoke screens to hide the real reason for his frustration, his loneliness, and his lostness.

This is the trick we play with a neurotic religion or an equally neurotic moralism, and one of the reasons some psychiatrists who see principally neurotic, abnormal people have come to believe that religion is good for nothing but the creation of more sick minds. What they and we need to remember is that the use of the virtues to exalt and justify ourselves is not religion at its best, certainly not the Christian religion, but rather a counterfeit of religion which must be understood and rejected along with a counterfeit morality.

Pride: Healthy and Unhealthy

"Pride is always wrong. Pride is a deadly sin; therefore, I will no longer be proud," one says. Thus he sets up a rigid principle of right behind which he may hide all manner of hurtful attitudes and acts. But pride is not always wrong. It is necessary and right that I should be proud of a good home, of my children's accomplishments, of the freedom and blessings of my country, of my own creative powers, and supremely of my relations to the mighty God of love and truth. Such pride is as healthy as the pride of "June bustin' out all over," as the lovely chorus from *Carousel* puts it. I ought to be "bustin' out all over" with pride before a waterfall, or a sunset, or a great symphony—the pride of being alive and part of this beautiful world! I ought to be rejoicing in my powers, as an athlete does in his prowess, or as a musician in his power to release a symphony in music, or an artist in his power to portray a scene of breath-taking beauty and meaning. How much we need this kind of pride!

But such healthy pride is worlds apart from the abnormal, destructive pride the Bible describes as the root of all sin—the twisted self-love and self-exaltation that causes us to set ourselves in the center and preen and worship ourselves and seek to have all others do so—the pride that seeks to be "as God" and to force others to recognize our exalted highness. When they fail to recognize and exalt us, we use their failure as an excuse to give way to envy, jealousy, anger, intolerance, hatred, lust, greed, and useless worry! [1]

Surely it is wrong to think too highly of ourselves; but it is just as wrong to think too lowly of ourselves. The country priest in Georges Bernanos' diary is counseling with a young woman whose lack of healthy pride had led her into endless difficulties and hurts. "It's a fine thing to rise above pride, but you must have pride in order to do so," he admonishes her. She expresses her surprise that a priest would recommend pride to her, "I never knew that pride was one of the theological virtues!" Then the young priest makes clear what he means:

I sometimes feel we're apt to belittle honour. We're all of us liable to lie down in the mud; it seems a cool, soft couch when hearts are jaded. And shame, you know, is a sleep like any other, a heavy sleep, a dreamless intoxication. . . . If a last shred of pride can stiffen the back of some wretched creature, why quibble about it? [2]

[1] See Chap. II, "Pride," in *Conquering the Seven Deadly Sins* (Nashville: Abingdon Press, 1955).

[2] *The Diary of a Country Priest*, tr. Pamela Morris (New York: The Macmillan Co., 1937), p. 224. Used by permission.

Why do we think too lowly of ourselves and so turn humility into a vice? Chiefly because we are doubtful of our own worth and lovableness, whether we consciously recognize it or not; and we are seeking to prove to ourselves and to others just how fine we really are. The easiest way to do this with the least cost, we think, is to major on being humble or unselfish.

Whatever it is in our previous experience that has caused us to doubt our own worth or lovableness—whether the rejection of parents or playmates or the ridicule of those who are "above us" in wealth or position—our insecurity causes us to say to ourselves and others, "I am a humble person." "I am very unselfish." The very same compulsive drive that causes some men to seek wealth and position may cause others to seek to excel in humility and unselfish service. So when I think, "I am very humble," it may really mean, "I am very proud of my humility—proud that I am not proud!" Coleridge says it so well:

> And the Devil did grin, for his darling sin
> Is pride that apes humility.

We smile as we read in one man's autobiography, "I have never lost the childish humility which characterizes all truly great men!" But we need to see ourselves in the mirror to realize how often we have twisted humility and even unselfishness to our own egoistic uses. Every one of us is insecure and doubtful of his worth at times and we have all chosen the way of self-deprecation and depreciation more than is healthy.

C. S. Lewis, in his *Screwtape Letters*, puts this insight into the words of the Devil's chief advocate, Screwtape, as he writes to one of his minor assistants, Wormwood, calling his attention to certain sayings that illustrate the importance of this method in carrying on the Devil's work: "If people knew how much ill-feeling Unselfishness occasions, it would not be so often recommended from the pulpit," and again, "She's the sort of woman who lives for others—you can always tell the others by their hunted expression!" [3]

We all know people who with the fabled Uriah Heep like to proclaim how unselfish they are. "If everyone were as unselfish as I, what a different world"—et cetera, et cetera, ad infinitum, ad nauseam! How often even those of us who work in the church or community organizations are tempted to give ourselves in the most unselfish ways, but always in the most noticeable places! And which of us parents has not, occasionally at least, succumbed to the temptation to remind his children of the sacrifices made on their behalf? "See how much I have done for you, how much I love you; therefore you should do as I say." Thus unselfish deeds, sacrificial giving, humble love, become a whip to make others do as we say. There is nothing more irritating or depressing than the consciously "humble" or "unselfish" person. It is exceedingly painful to be around him.

D. H. Lawrence tells this story of two sisters: Ursula, "slapped by her sister Theresa, in a mood of Christian humility silently presented the other side of her face which Theresa, in exasperation at the challenge, also hit. Whereupon Ursula with *boiling* heart went meekly away." [4]

Such meekness is neither Christian nor is it humble. No wonder the author comments, "There is something unclean and degrading about the humble side of Christianity." For, of course, if this were the true meaning of Christian humility, we would all have to despise it. "The virtue's final taint is the condescension of the conscious saint!" There is nothing more unlovely and despicable, nothing more difficult to swallow, than the *self-righteousness* of that kind of virtue! Such forgiveness and mercy is harder to forgive than vengeance and open cruelty. And yet, which of us, whether we profess to be Christian or not, has not at times given what we thought was mercy or even forgiveness condescendingly? "Surely

[3] (New York: The Macmillan Co., 1943), pp. 134-35.
[4] *The Rainbow* (New York: Albert & Charles Boni, 1930), p. 268. Italics mine.

I forgive you, you poor fool—so low beneath me—it really doesn't matter!"

But this is not genuine Christlike humility and forgiveness, as revealed so triumphantly in Jesus and in those who have caught his spirit. His "turning the other cheek" was not used as a weapon to show how superior he was. He turned the other cheek in sincere love for the other person—an outgoing, affirmative love that did not stop even at the cross. His going the second mile was not primarily to rebuke those who compelled him, but a positive act of genuine concern for the unjust person that in many cases opened the door to new life for him. There is absolutely no condescension in the love that came down from the cross. He suffered, was hurt, was heartbroken; but he identified himself with the sinners and with those who crucified him. They knew he cared and cared deeply for them. This was the moving power behind his prayer, "Forgive them; for they know not what they do." (See Matt. 5 and Luke 23.) Such humility and unselfishness, such forgiveness and mercy, are good if they are not filled with self-pity and the corresponding desire for self-exaltation. And such freedom to love in all circumstances is possible only for him who is himself secure in the Love that endures all earthly storms of hate, passion, and human frailty.

II. Love Needs No Escape from Inadequacy

Again, true humility and unselfishness—which result from self-acceptance—are lost and twisted when they become excuses for or escapes from feelings of inadequacy. All of us have such feelings. It is the nature of our finiteness to feel our inferiority before the vast demands of life and the universe. How can we be adequate in the swift passage of time, with such threatening dangers as ill health, economic and social insecurity, old age, and death? Some of us feel it more than others, depending on the kinds of pressure put on us since childhood. Some meet these feelings of inadequacy and

24

inferiority by acting the opposite: by frank, open, sometimes showy attempts at superiority—by making a big name, amassing great wealth, by becoming a braggart—forcing a success that never quite believes in itself. Others, by practicing humility and self-depreciation in the presence of others, hope to accomplish the same purpose: namely, to build up their self-confidence.

Edna Ferber, in her autobiography, describes her terrific feelings of inadequacy as a writer—"which made me feel that all other writers were superior to me." She did not have confidence in her own ability and hungered for some way to prove to herself that she was not inferior. So when someone would say with real sincerity, "I like your McChesney stories, they're great," she would reply, "Oh, do you really! I thought the last one was quite bad. I don't know anything about traveling salesmen, anyway. It wasn't about anything, really." [5] Her humility was only the means by which she sought the praise of others. Who of us has not practiced this kind of humility? After doing something or making something, we depreciate it, anxiously hoping that those who hear our depreciation will pile on the praise. We run ourselves down in order to hear others, in the interest of justice, run us up! We think that if we put a low enough estimate on ourselves, surely others will come along and raise the estimate and make us feel better!

There is always the danger that such self-depreciation may put us in the position of the man with an inferiority complex who went to the psychiatrist, telling him how inferior he felt. After the second visit the psychiatrist dismissed him. Someone asked the man what the psychiatrist had said, and he answered in disgust, "He told me that I *am* inferior!" The story doubtless has been invented; yet the answer of the psychiatrist is terribly true: for the law of our minds declares that what gets our attention gets us, and if we repeat to others and to ourselves often enough that we are inadequate and inferior, surely we will be. "I'm convinced," writes one great spirit, "I have never had enough self-confidence.

[5] *A Peculiar Treasure* (New York: Doubleday & Co., 1939), p. 182.

To doubt oneself is not to be humble, I even think that sometimes it is the most hysterical form of pride, a pride almost delirious, a kind of jealous ferocity which makes an unhappy man turn and rend himself. That must be the real truth of hell." [6]

Such self-doubting is commonplace with most of us moderns. We may not like to admit it to ourselves; but here is our deepest and most terrifying problem: Am I able to do what I must do to have real life? Am I able to face the possibilities of failure, pain, old age, and death? The results of our self-doubting are seen in the hurt we do to our bodies and to our minds as well as to others.

Courageous Humility

True humility is not self-depreciation or self-abasement, but self-acceptance and self-dedication in the highest sense of the word. It is not selling yourself long, nor is it selling yourself short. It is openness before the real truth about your life and your situation, with utter confidence that the real truth about you contains elements of grandeur and strength worthy of the dedication and concentration of all your attention.

Such humility comes only in the perspective of faith in the goodness at the heart of our universe, which is what we mean when we as Christians say we believe in "God, the Father of our Lord Jesus Christ." That some men and women of all the high religions have possessed this humility is an indication that there are also genuine elements of truth in these avenues of faith. There is not space here for a discussion of comparative religions. It is enough to say that the Christian religion and the Hebrew faith upon which it was founded describe the nature of Ultimate Reality in the beautiful words of the 108th psalm:

> I will sing, I will sing praises!
>
> . . . .
>
> For thy steadfast love is great above the heavens,
>   thy faithfulness reaches to the clouds!

[6] Bernanos, *op. cit.*, p. 249.

The Christian faith goes on to see this steadfast, faithful love revealed, illustrated, and vindicated in the life and death and resurrection of the Christ, thereby providing for us the clearest light and firmest foundation for a healthy perspective of life that we know.

True humility comes to the person standing on the Rock of Ages where the eternal light of the steadfast love of God in Christ shines upon him. In moments of clear insight and high worship, such a one can say, with the writer of I John 3:

See what love the Father has given us, that we should be called children of God; and so we are. The reason why the world does not know us is that it did not know him. Beloved, we are God's children now; it does not yet appear what we shall be, but we know that when he appears we shall be like him, for we shall see him as he is. And every one who thus hopes in him purifies himself as he is pure.

The exact meaning of being "children of God" can never be described or adequately defined in human, earthly terms because it represents our spiritual relationships which can only be symbolized. This does not in any sense lessen the value of the reality thus represented but rather deepens our sense of the mystery and glory of life. It can be illustrated best in this analogy which Jesus used of children loved by the Father. It is enough to say of the Creative Spirit in whom we live and move and have our being, as he said:

If you then, who are evil, know how to give good gifts to your children, how much more will the heavenly Father give the Holy Spirit [resulting in love and peace and confidence] to those who ask him. (Luke 11:13.)

The words of Sir John Bowring put it as adequately as any outside the Bible:

> God is love; His mercy brightens
> All the path in which we rove;

27

> Bliss He wakes and woe He lightens:
> God is wisdom, God is love!

Humility, which is simply the acceptance of the real self, therefore has its roots deep in the heart of Eternal Love, which has made us and bought us and kept us as cherished and beloved members of a blessed family of brothers and sisters. It is an amazing thing to believe that there is a real spiritual relationship between the Almighty God and me; and especially is this so when I see how unworthily and carelessly I have lived. To believe in this spiritual relationship does not require a visualization of God as a big man, but it does demand the opening of my heart by faith to the infinite possibilities of my personal life as well as the life of humanity, for "it does not yet appear what we shall be, but we know . . . we shall be like him."

As he thinks of the treasure of our faith in Everlasting Love, Pascal writes:

> There must be feelings of greatness, not from merit, but from grace, and after having passed through humiliation. . . . The knowledge of God without that of men's misery causes pride. The knowledge of man's misery without that of God causes despair. The knowledge of Jesus Christ constitutes the middle course, because in Him we find both God and our misery. . . . Jesus Christ is a God whom we approach without pride, and before whom we humble ourselves without despair! [7]

That is, in him we see a revelation of man at his highest, and of God as wise, loving Father-spirit, which is the highest any human being can conceive. God is like Christ and our humanity is meant to grow into the maturity of this kind of noble life, "in his likeness." (Cf. Phil. 3:17-21.) This is the faith that results in hope and love.

[7] Blaise Pascal, *Pensées*, tr. W. F. Trotter (New York: Random House, 1941), pars. 524, 526, and 527.

The best way to be humble with self-confidence and strength is to stand thankfully by faith in the presence of God, whose wise and loving providence makes it possible to believe that there are infinite possibilities ahead for you. You are accepted and loved by God, not because of your worthiness, not because you have proved yourself lovable and good, or strong and adequate, but because God is love, and you, his creature-child, are chosen as the object of his love. Here is the great and worthy purpose of prayer and worship: "Practicing the presence of God." Self-acceptance with the ability to love yourself properly is one of the by-products. "The true way to be humble," said Phillips Brooks, "is not to stoop until you are smaller than yourself, but to stand at your real height against some higher nature that will show you what the real smallness of your greatness is!" You and I are great—called to be the sons and daughters of God! But as you stand in his presence, you see the smallness of your greatness and you do not become inordinately proud. You accept yourself for what you are.

The Creative Power of Self-Acceptance

How precious is the freedom and joy of self-acceptance! For there is in each of us so much more capacity and character than we know. The fact that it is still only potential does not mean it is not there, any more than the rushing waters of Niagara are considered worthless because there is no dynamo to convert their potential energy into power. Learning to trust and love our true selves in the framework of a serene trust and acceptance of the love of the Eternal is the dynamo that can convert our potential into actual. If the average person realizes only one twentieth of his possibilities, how precious then is the opening of our minds to see the other nineteen twentieths and putting our attention upon it!

This is true humility. It accepts the amazing love of God for me and gives to me, as it did to Bernadette, the little maid of Lourdes, "an acute and soberly accurate estimate of the self," which neither the criticism nor the praises of the world can shake, nor the failures that come upon me can destroy.

It is significant that those who have contributed the most to their world have possessed this kind of strong humility. Said William Pitt, in an hour of great darkness for his beloved Britain, "I believe I can save England and I am the only one who can." Here was a pride that was truly humble. He knew his powers and was able to use them. "Trust thyself," cried Emerson; "every heart vibrates to that iron string!"

III. Love Needs No Cover-up for Failures

What we need is the courage to accept ourselves, not only with all our limitations and failures, but also with all our divinely given possibilities, and then to become ourselves in steady fulfillment of these powers. Again, therefore, what we sometimes call humility may become a deadly vice instead of a virtue when it is an excuse for lack of courage. Instead of supplying us with courage, it prevents us from finding and using it.

As a boy, one of my favorite stories in the Old Testament was the story of twelve spies who were sent by Moses to spy out the Promised Land before the children of Israel attempted to take it. They returned with glowing pictures of the riches of the Promised Land; but all except two of them were frightened out of their wits. "We saw giants . . . ," gasped the ten. "We seemed to ourselves like grasshoppers, and so we seemed to them."

How pitiable that humility is so often associated with a confession of weakness and is used as a cloak to cover our fears! How many of us know only the barren wastes of weasel living and petty accomplishment, when the promised land flowing with the milk and honey of creative living is waiting for us! Our false humility simply gives further justification to our fears: "We are unable . . . we see giants . . . we are as grasshoppers!" And we hate ourselves for it. We would give anything to match the giants and to go over into the promised land, but we can't. We are disgusted with ourselves, and cloak our self-disgust even from ourselves by our humility, or as in the case of the young Irishwoman, by our several conquests or by our greedy acquisitions. This attitude is indeed the final vice. It is certainly not the humility of a mature person, who rejects such shabby self-disgust, such a "brow-beaten, dog-slinging attitude" as unworthy of his stature as a child of God.

The Source of Courage

The person with true humility believes in the infinite glories of God's resources for himself and his world. This he believes in spite of the evils of man's blindness and selfishness that seem to make an atomic war inevitable. As he looks at the long millenniums of struggle from what biologists call the primeval slime, he sees in evolution, or in whatever method we scientific-minded folk believe man came into being, the purposive creative hand of an Everlasting Love that has brought us to the edge of discoveries in human living that will far eclipse the victories of the human spirit thus far.

The work of a distinguished biochemist and biophysicist, Pierre Lecomte du Noüy, traces the growth of man from purely animal life with obedience only to animal laws of self-preservation, etc., to the heights of human nobility and self-sacrifice, which contradicts all his former animal tendencies. This, he says, is the best evidence to the scientific mind of the action of God as loving purpose in the universe, and gives us confidence in the greatness of human destiny.[8]

An atomic war could come. The inevitable *progress* of *this* civilization the man of humility knows to be an illusion. But his faith in the Almighty God of everlasting love gives him *hope;* and in this hope he is not ashamed to believe and to seek for the way by which this Eternal Love may be translated into human love in the moment of existence, day by day, in his own world. He is sure that his own powers and the possibilities of his universe are filled with undiscovered wonders waiting for his confident action. In

[8] See *Human Destiny* (New York: Longmans, Green & Co., 1947).

this spirit he continually "asks . . . seeks . . . knocks" and finds increasingly great his powers to endure, to create, to love, and to live! Jesus was describing this kind of person when he said, "Blessed are the meek, for they shall inherit the earth."

The Powerful Meek

But how we have twisted this word "meek." To the average American, meekness is a symbol of weakness because it is thought of as passive instead of the active, creative passion for truth and goodness which Jesus said would inherit the earth. The Greek word comes from the same root as the word used to describe the willingness of oxen yoked together to pull a load. To be meek means to be willing to work together with God in the discovery and acceptance of truth and in obedience to our highest possibilities. It means "good will toward man and reverent obedience toward God." [9] I am truly meek only as I accept my real status and stature in the love of God and man.

Robert Frost was meek when for twenty years, month after month, he received only rejection slips for his writing, but his meekness was not an excuse for quitting. It was rather an open-minded appraisal of his powers, of his desire to write creatively, of the reasons for the poor quality of his work, and a fresh determination to meet and conquer the Giants in the Promised Land of Creative Writing. That he became one of America's most loved and respected poets is a tribute to his powerful meekness. He could have said, as the rejection slips kept coming, "I guess it just isn't in me to write," or, "The critics and publishers are blind and unfair; therefore I'll quit." To have done so would have resulted in a self-hate that would have closed the door on any outgoing love for others. Failure would have made him bitter, cynical, hating others, as it has so many people, but his faith in God and in himself and in his love of writing and of people made him strong.

[9] George A. Buttrick, *The Interpreter's Bible,* VII (Nashville: Abingdon Press, 1951), 282.

Every scientist is meek who fails and comes back for one more try, saying in the spirit of Edison, "We have not failed; we have only found nine hundred and ninety-nine ways that won't work." The wonders of this physical universe have been explored and developed by men who believed that there was a way that would open the door to them. What is needed now, more than anything else, is for countless men and women to be humbly meek before the truths of our personal and social universe, believing that God has the way to peace and well-being for us rather than destruction, and that seeking courageously, we shall find it! Whether the scientist acknowledges it or not, he who stands humbly before the truth, seeking it with ardor and enthusiasm, confesses to his confidence in the Eternal Goodness, which is Divine Love.

I can close my eyes and see a long procession of discouraged, self-hating men and women who have come into my study through the years. They had been driven by their foolish pride which made them attempt the achievement of impossible goals. Their false pride was indeed a "jealous ferocity," causing their unhappy souls to turn and rend themselves. They felt inferior, inadequate, and were bitterly angry and disgusted with themselves and with God because they were not superior and adequate. Not all continued in this sorry state. Some of them took a fresh look at themselves in the mirror of the love of God and began to see their true greatness, hidden and covered by so many years of self-hating. And on this Rock of Humility they began to walk with a courage that faced all the storms of failure and reverses that make up life. From my own experience with them, I know it is grandly true that the humble meek do possess the earth! Not necessarily in fee simple, but in the spirit of joyful, confident victory!

IV. Love Meets Guilt Creatively

No, the virtue of true humility, or unselfishness, or any other virtue is not a means of showing our superiority over others, or of hiding our own feelings of inadequacy, or of excusing our failures

33

and lack of courage. Neither is it a means of escaping from the sense of guilt, which is the most difficult part of our failures and wrongs to overcome. And yet this is the most oft-used method of dealing with guilt.

"At moments she discovered she was grotesquely wrong; she treated herself to a week of passionate humility," thus Henry James describes one of his characters. But her humility was humiliation, and humiliation itself is good for no one. It is certainly not desired by God. Kicking yourself when you fail or do wrong is a futile dissipation indeed. Many of us are not aware that we have such resentment toward ourselves, but all of us have it to some extent when we fail or make mistakes. It is difficult for our prideful selves to accept the fact that "to err is human." Instead, we defend and excuse our errors and failures before others and condemn ourselves unmercifully to ourselves. "Self-hate is pride's inseparable companion and [a person] cannot have one without the other," declares Karen Horney, psychotherapist. Here indeed pride is a deadly sin. No one can love others until first of all he loves himself—not the false, little, prideful self, but the true self that God sees in him and that he can become. "Love requires that a man be *more* of a self, not less; and it gives him the power to do it." [10]

Humility is not kicking yourself when you do wrong, but rather the facing of your wrong, the accepting of forgiveness, and the beginning of a new and different life. To treat yourself to an hour, or a week, or a year, or a lifetime of "passionate humility" is to leave yourself weaker and less of a person than before. To accept God's forgiveness does not mean self-abasement. It means self-cleansing and self-dedication to a new life. It means standing on this Rock of Reality, seeing and admitting your weaknesses, wrongs, and failures, knowing that they are forgiven by God, forgiving yourself, and turning with joy toward the infinite possibilities of the present and the future.

[10] E. La B. Cherbonnier, *Hardness of Heart* (Garden City, N. Y.: Doubleday & Co., 1955), p. 116.

How does one accept the forgiveness of God and become willing to forgive himself? Not by any amount of masochistic browbeating or self-loathing! This is further to defile yourself as God's beloved child. Only by seeking to understand why and how you did the wrong thing and failed, and then thinking no more about the past as you take up the infinite good that streams into your present from the hands of Eternal Love. Only thus is forgiveness given and received. The good may be difficult to see, because you are so accustomed to your own narrow perspective, but it is there once you are done with self-abasement and self-loathing.

Such humility and forgiveness are the most powerful, the most creative, and the most beautiful experiences of which the human spirit is capable. Not that you can make yourself worthy of such forgiveness and new power, but that you are being made worthy for this glorious new freedom through him who loved you and gave himself for you.

Before real love is possible in you, you must accept yourself by faith as loved by the God of love. The self-centered "I" must go, but only as there is a Divine Love that enables you to see it and surrender it. You cannot command yourself to be at peace. You cannot make yourself quit worrying. Neither can you make yourself love. You can't get rid of the self-demanding, self-despising "I" by your own powers. You lose it only as you look into the light of Eternal Love and are lifted out of yourself, forgiven and freed, able to become your true self.

This is what Paul meant when he said: "Now we see through a glass, darkly [in a mirror dimly]; but then face to face: now I know in part; but then shall I know even as also I am known" (I Cor. 13:12 K.J.V.). He was talking about the mirror of Jesus Christ, by which we may see, through faith and prayer, the goodness and love of God. When we look at Christ in our prayers of adoration, surrender, and trust, it is like looking into a mirror and seeing the love of God but dimly compared to what we will see. Look often enough and sincerely enough even though your vision is dim and you will be "mastered by the love of Christ." Then it will be true of you as of Paul that "the very spring of our actions is the love of Christ" (II Cor. 5:15 Phillips).

The fact is that any person who is unable to share wise outgoing love with others has never received this mighty redeeming love that God is waiting to give him!

Grace N., whose story began this chapter, had never really known the security of accepting herself as loved by God, as forgiven and worth while. She was too self-despising and therefore too hostile toward others because nobody would give her the love she felt she deserved. She needed help from someone who knew God's love and could share it with her, not only in words but in wise, strong attitudes and acts—a psychiatrist—a pastor—a friend— yes, but ultimately her deep need could be met only by the love of God shining in the face of Jesus Christ, and in those who reveal his spirit. How right Elsa Barker was in saying:

> He who knows God's love—becomes love, and his eyes
> Behold Love in the heart of everyone,
> Even the Loveless: as the light of the sun
> Is one with all it touches. . . [11]

Paul was mastered by the love of Christ when he saw it shining in the eyes of Stephen, the young Christian martyr for whose death Paul was responsible. Before then, he was the self-centered Saul, hostile toward the world and himself because he could not get all the approval and recognition he wanted. He stood and watched the love in Stephen, as dying he prayed, "Do not hold this sin against them." Then Saul met the love of Christ and became Paul. The self-centered "I" was transformed and now Christ was living through him. Then he was able to write about and live the life of agape or giving-love.

It was this experience which gave rise to one of the best-loved

[11] Used by permission.

hymns of Christendom, "Rock of Ages." The author, Augustus M. Toplady, must have been fighting himself as well as the storms of failure and wrong. In discouragement and self-disgust he wandered one day to the seashore, where he watched the mighty waves of the sea crash time and again on the sides of a huge rock on which he stood. After each fresh onslaught of raging fury, the rock was still there as strong as ever. We do not know the course of his thoughts in that moment, but I like to imagine that he was meditating on the words of Ps. 40, in which the singer declares that God has "set my feet upon a rock, making my steps secure," or perhaps it was Ps. 18:

> I love thee, O Lord, my strength.
> The Lord is my rock, and my fortress, and my deliverer!

Something happened in that hour which resulted in a new strength and power for Augustus Toplady. Writing in a magazine published in 1775, he gives an inkling of what it was, as he counsels others:

Yet if you fall, be humbled; do not despair. Pray afresh to God, who is able so to raise you up and set you on your feet again. . . . Say to the Lord from the depth of your heart:

> Rock of Ages, cleft for me,
> Let me hide myself in Thee.
>
> . . . . . .
>
> Could my tears forever flow,
> Could my zeal no languor know,
> These for sin could not atone.
> Thou must save, and Thou alone:
> In my hand no price I bring,
> Simply to Thy cross I cling!

Yes, you and I conquer our self-doubting and self-hating pride and anxiety when we accept ourselves just as we are, standing on that Eternal Rock, with the light of the gracious, steadfast love of God shining upon us! The only lasting joy and freedom of life begins when I escape the prisoning walls of inordinate self-love, which is nothing more than self-doubting and the corresponding attempt at self-proving, and the inevitable self-hatred that results. Such joy is mine when I enter by faith into union with the Love who dwells and sings within me and every one of my fellows, when I am willing to listen to his divine music and share it with others. Then I am able to be *present* with my fellows, not just "beside them"—for this could mean being "outside them." Instead I am truly *"with* them." *Then I am completely myself.*

III. Learning to Give Love

To be loved by God is life's highest privilege, but we need more than the love of God. We also long hungrily to be loved by other persons: the members of our family, our friends and neighbors, the people with whom we work.

Before we can be loved, we must learn how to love others. We have too often considered our problem as one of making ourselves lovable—*how to be loved;* whereas, the place to begin is—*how to love.* The chief occupation of many of us is "How to win friends and influence people"—how to be lovable. Women attempt to make themselves beautiful and attractive by cultivating their bodies, dress, and manner. Men attempt to become successful, wealthy, powerful, strong, well-dressed. Our worst nightmares, whether asleep or awake, are due to the fear that we are somehow not lovable, that we cannot find and keep the love of others.

"The supreme happiness in life is the conviction that we are loved," wrote Victor Hugo. Certainly most people would agree. Not so, say the wisest of modern doctors, who realize the truth of Jesus' words, "It is better to give than receive." They are saying with Jesus and the apostle Paul that *the supreme happiness in life is the ability to* give *love!*

Two Kinds of Love

We must first understand clearly the difference between giving-love and desiring-love as defined in the first chapter. Giving love to others as God gives love to us is a wholehearted, spontaneous response that is wisely courageous in helping those we love to new worth and value which they otherwise could not have.

Desiring-love is the conditional, possessive, acquisitive response

39

I make to others who I feel deserve my love. As long as they deserve it and give me what I want, help me, exalt me, I love them; but when they cease to deserve it, my love is killed. Such love ends. Period. Nothing can resurrect it, except if and when the one desiring my love proves his or her worthiness and becomes again lovable in my eyes.

Giving-love is a real outgoing of myself to another self. The union that results may be described as an "I-Thou" relationship of mutual respect, reverence, and concern, a sense of responsibility for each other. On the other hand, the desiring-love that seeks to acquire another person or some good from that person can only enter into an "I-It" relationship.[1] The one I love becomes a thing to be used and owned, manipulated for my own satisfaction or success. Giving-love alone makes life beautiful. It is this kind of love which Paul described in his classic Hymn to Love:

> Love is patient and kind;
> Love is not jealous or boastful;
> It is not arrogant or rude.
> Love does not insist on its own way;
> It is not irritable or resentful;
> It does not rejoice at wrong,
> But rejoices in the right.
>
> Love bears all things,
> Believes all things,
> Hopes all things,
> Endures all things.
>
> .   .   .   .
>
> So faith, hope, love abide, these three;
> But the greatest of these is love.
> —I Cor. 13:4-13

[1] Cf. Martin Buber, *I and Thou*, tr. Ronald Gregor Smith (New York: Charles Scribner's Sons, 1937), pp. 3-34.

The whole truth is that the summit of great living is reached only when two kinds of love, giving-love and possessing-love, are joined together. As the Indian poet Kabir puts it:

> Subtle is the path of love. . . . Therein there is no
> asking and no not-asking!

The emphasis, however, must be put on giving-love, or all true love is lost.

"Remember that love is not getting, but giving," exclaims Henry Van Dyke; "not a wild dream of pleasure and a madness of desire—oh, no, love is not that; and it is the best thing in the world and the thing that lives longest."

Acquisitive, possessive love always fails to win another's love, or even respect. This is the thing that many people simply cannot understand. When you say, "Prove your love for me by doing what I want," you are using your love as a whip and it will be deeply resented and resisted. You are treating me as an "it" to be used, manipulated, acquired. To say as a lover, or a parent, or a husband or wife, "You belong to me—I love you; therefore you do as I say," is almost the kiss of death for real love. It may survive, but it will be hurt and weakened. But he who surrenders his demands that others show their love for him by serving and exalting him, who gives genuine, outgoing love without demanding anything in return, is the only one who, in the long run, is likely to be loved with any deeply enriching love. For when I am unable to give love, I am also unable to accept it; and the more I demand it, the less I am able to receive it.

The moving picture *Serenade* contrasts the difference between the two kinds of love in the story of the way two women loved a young singer, Damon Vincent. Kendall Hale, a spoiled, utterly self-centered woman of wealth "discovered" the young singer in a vineyard, and in her own words "made a singer out of him." "He is like one of my masks—he belongs to me." Having been lifted by her out of obscurity and supposedly given her love, the young singer soon discovered that she wanted him and his success as just another proof of her power. She loved him as an "it," a thing to use and gloat over. She cared no more for him than for others whom she had "made." Vincent was hurt deeply by her fickleness and possessiveness. Unable to sing, not caring to live, he fled to Mexico, where he was saved from destroying himself by the love of young Juana Montes, the daughter of a rancher. She took pity on him at first, and then giving herself wholeheartedly to him, she described how she loved him, "What is best for Damon, that is my concern!" Through the inspiration of her faith in God and her own generous love for him, he began to accept himself and found the will to sing again. He discovered that the will to sing, like the will to love, was given by the acceptance of the divine love shining through the love of this beautiful person.

The Failure of Purely Romantic Love

Here is the reason for the failure of most romantic love. It is utterly self-centered. Moonlight! Soft music! Strong desire! You love. You get married. You are supposed to be happy; but you are not! Why? Because you cannot utterly *possess* the other person, so you become jealous, envious. You insist on your own way. If he loved you, *he* would make *you* happy!

You feel your pulse every few minutes to see how happy you are and finally you give it up as a bad job. You don't love him any more, because he is so unloving toward you and therefore so unlovable. You call it quits and give as an excuse "incompatibility"! The real reason for many marital failures is the fact that one or both parties have a compulsive need for love. They must prove their own lovableness, and therefore they seek to possess the other as love slaves, whose chief purpose in life is to exalt and glorify their partner's ego.

Life is not built that way. It is giving-love alone that makes life full and rich and satisfying. When your love is unconditioned by what the other does or does not do for you; when you give without demanding in return; when you love not only when the other person is easily lovable and obviously worth helping but even when he is a "stinker," unworthy and unlovable, when you see him as valuable to you as he is to God; then it is that your love may help God create within him something that is truly worthy and lovable.

What a horrible twist romantic love, as sung by twentieth-century groaners and crooners, has taken. "You *belong* to me . . . I *belong* to you!" Romantic love has its place, but only as it is followed by or included in a wise Christlike love for each other. There is a sense in which belonging to each other can be a rich and precious experience. "He who turns to the other human being and opens himself to him receives the world in him, and when they say to one another, 'It is Thou,' the indwelling of God is between them." [2] But when the emphasis is on "you belong to *me*," the deep meaning of love is reversed and the relation becomes demonic.

They say that love is blind! Not so. Love sees deeper and further than any self-centered ego can ever see. Giving-love sees with God and goes to the limits to help the one loved become his best self. There may come a time when through the complete unresponsiveness of the other, the relationship of marriage can no longer endure; but in a large majority of cases, giving-love does bring a response that can set the marriage on new foundations of spiritual understanding and co-operation.[3] This I know from experience through the years in counseling with numerous couples whose marriages were breaking up on the rocks of self-centered possessing-love. I have seen the hard shells of bitterness and resentment broken by the touch of real love. I have seen miracles of reunion begin and continue, so that a seemingly hopeless and

[2] Buber, *op. cit.*
[3] See Chap. VIII for a treatment on love and justice in the problem of divorce.

43

incompatible marriage finds the foundations for deep harmony and success, but always under the disciplines of giving-love.

"When you love someone deeply enough anything can happen!" Thus the lovely Scotch lassie declares her confidence to the young American lover in the musical comedy *Brigadoon*.

Giving-love does make miracles happen, first of all to you who give the love and also to the one to whom it is given. It is nature's way of making "out of three sounds, not a fourth, but a star." Only when two marriage partners love each other in the spirit of agape love are they lifted out of self-centeredness and into a union that brings something of heaven down to earth. The same is true not only of love between friends but of love for all mankind.

Jesus' beatitudes do not say, "Blessed are the ones who are loved," but rather, "Blessed are you even though you are persecuted, unloved, and hurt, because as sons of your Father in heaven you will be able to be peacemakers in many situations, and where you cannot bring peace to others, you will have a courageous peace in your own heart! Therefore, rejoice when men say evil against you!"

This paraphrase of the teachings of Jesus in the Sermon on the Mount indicates the way in which the miracles of giving-love can and do take place in our human relations.

How do I give the wise, Godlike love that never fails? This is the practical question to which this chapter is dedicated. The chapters that follow will seek to apply this answer to several of the areas of our human life, where the giving-Christlike-love may prevent true goodness from being so easily spoiled and lost without our realizing it.

There are three sure tests of genuine giving-love which may point the way:

1. It faces reality rather than seeking to escape it.
2. It goes beyond sentimentality to a genuine concern for the well-being of the ones loved.

3. It sets the loved ones free rather than enslaving them.

When your love can pass these tests, then it is that you are most likely to be loved. "Give and it will be given unto you!" cried Jesus.

> Give love and love to your heart will flow!
> A strength for your every need.[4]

I. Giving-Love Faces Reality

Love that heals, cultivates, protects, and inspires must first of all enable the one loved to face reality rather than seek to escape from it. Love is cruel and hurtful when it is unintelligent, lacking in understanding concerning the results of its actions. It is a healing force when it becomes the motivating power in helping those loved to see things as they are and to act accordingly.

Unintelligent love may be either soft or harsh. Soft love, notwithstanding the best of intentions, may be the more cruel of the two. "I love you and therefore do not want you to struggle, suffer, or have a hard time" may be the most unkind words I could say to you. In seeking to shield you from the suffering necessary to growth and maturity, I may prevent you from coming to grips with the truth about life and thus defer the day when you will be able to meet it with insight and victory.

The mother of Paul Burgess, in A. J. Cronin's *Beyond This Place*, thought she was showing her love for her son when she kept from him until he was a grown young man the fact that his father was in prison for murder and that his name was not Paul Burgess but Paul Mathry.

"Why?" Paul asked.

"I wanted to forget that name," she answered. "I wanted you to be out of sight and sound of it forever!"

"But why?" Paul kept asking.

---

[4] Ella Wheeler Wilcox. Used by permission of Rand McNally & Co.

There was a pause. Her eyes fell. Almost inaudibly she answered: "To save you . . . from a horrible shame!" [5]

But the shame the young man felt then was infinitely greater than any suffering he could have borne had she faced him with the facts through the years. The story relates Paul's terrific battle, not only to clear the name of his father, but to win for himself a strong, independent character. His success came in spite of his mother's soft love rather than because of it. In the end it was obvious that his mother's love was cruel, both for her son and her husband!

Soft Desiring-Love

Even kindness may be unkind when it keeps a person from meeting the real truth of a given situation wherein something rigorous and unyielding is called for. As Jacques Barzun in *Teacher in America* puts it, "Most of the heart-burnings in the academic world come from somebody's yielding to the temptation to be kind at the wrong time!" The teacher whose love for her students is really kind and strong is not the one who continually lets them get by with shoddy work or with wrong attitudes. The teachers we each cherish from our school days are beloved for the simple reason that they refused the temptation to be "kind" at the wrong times.

One of the most successful teachers I ever met was a little thing, physically. But she taught a room full of overgrown boys with great skill and effectiveness. One of her boys was asked, "How could such a little thing as your teacher manage to teach you big boys anything?" He answered with words that were understood by all who knew her, "She knows how to make us sit down with our consciences!"

The mother who shelters her children from responsibility and the father who helps his son out of one scrape after another are simply postponing the day when they must face the results of ir-

* (Boston: Little, Brown & Co., 1953), p. 11.

responsibility and the penalty of wrong attitudes and acts. Children spoiled by false kindness are the ones whose delinquency is the most difficult to remove. The records of any juvenile court, as well as the courts before which our success in life is judged, reveal the pitiable failures of parents who get their sons or daughters out of trouble time and time again until they are at last in trouble from which no one can extricate them. It is not kindness, nor is it love, to give our children everything they want, to spoil them by removing all trouble and struggle, so that they never know how to use their wings.

"Momism" is the name given by Edward Strecker to this soft but vicious attitude.[6] As a psychiatrist he had ample opportunity, not only in his own private practice but in the psychoneurotic wards of the army, to see the curse placed on their children by parents who fail "to prepare [their] offspring emotionally for living a productive adult life." Strecker believes "momism" is at the root of many crack-ups in the army as in all areas of life. "In about 80 percent of the alcoholic cases I have studied, momism in childhood was the basic, underlying cause!" The term "mom" is not used here derisively—there are some wonderful mothers with strong, mature love who are called "Mom" by their families. It is a term used to designate the kind of mother who claims to be "giving up her life" for her children, but who is really seeking emotional compensation "for the buffets which life has dealt her own ego. Hidden from public view, however, is the hard and tragic fact that for the lives 'they give' for their children, they exact in return either directly—or even more destructively, indirectly—the emotional lives of their children." [7]

Yet there are endless illustrations in the lives of those about us of the success met by those who know how to love. I think of one

[6] The term "momism" has also been used by Philip Wylie and others.

[7] See Edward A. Strecker, *Their Mothers' Sons* (rev. ed.; Philadelphia: J. B. Lippincott Co., 1951), pp. 30, 122.

father who longed to keep his daughter from being hurt by "over-privileges" of too much and too easy, which seem so unavoidable in families of means. He had been brought up in poverty as to material things, but his parents had left him a wealth of courage and wisdom for using his talents creatively. How could he leave his daughter the same heritage under such different circumstances? First he determined to teach her that "things" are not as valuable as the spirit with which they are used. One day when she was only fourteen, she wanted a fur coat. He could very easily have bought her the most expensive one available. Instead he encouraged her to get a job in the summer and work for it. He explained to her that a fur coat is a luxury which very few grown women enjoy. It was all right for her to have one, but she needed to know its value and cost so that she would truly appreciate wearing it. Besides, he believed her experience in working for it would be worth more than the coat! Naturally she questioned his wisdom —thought him rather hard-hearted, as adolescents often feel toward parents who are firm. Nevertheless, she found a job, and years later realized what a priceless thing he had done for her. She had learned to appreciate things of infinitely greater value than a fur coat—things that no one could *give* her!

In matters other than financial, we may fail our children by being too easy on them. Why would a parent fail to teach his children to take responsibility? The excuse may be "to make it easier for them—they have so many lessons." The real reason is found in the oft-heard statement, "It's easier to do it myself." That is, they are thinking primarily of their own ease. It is not an indication of love for the children but of love for their own convenience.

We need to remember that *everything* we do for and with those we love gives them either more or less independence, self-confidence, patience, and sense of responsibility. A continuous, disciplined review of our attitudes in conversation at the table, in the process of carrying out the practical relationships that make up daily living, and in the approach to big and little problems is supremely important. The unexamined life is likely to be the unloving life. Prayer and worship afford the best opportunities for seeing the quality of our attempts at loving, for showing us ways to correct our mistakes and for learning to share our power of loving with others.

Families, with or without children, who accept the bountiful gifts of our American prosperity and live as little self-centered islands without being concerned with the sufferings and needs outside their island, do not love each other with intelligent realism. Why? Because they are treating each other to the soft love of selfishness, wherein ease is considered more important than character, and wherein life's true joys and meaning cannot be found. A further treatment of this need for overflowing concern and love for others outside our self-centered island will be found in Chaps. IV and V.

Harsh Love

The opposite extreme in the name of love is to be so harsh and domineering in the discipline of our loved ones that they fail to see the good we intend for them. The wisdom of the Creator is revealed in our innate reaction against being dominated. This is true whether it be children reacting against overdominant parents or Southerners reacting against what is regarded as dictatorship from Northerners concerning their association with the colored race. Even when we know that the goal others seek to force upon us is good, we may fight back, and in fighting reject the good. In the name of love, the authoritarian parent or husband or wife or friend may destroy the very thing he sets out to gain!

Some authority, some discipline, is necessary, obviously, in the case of the young; but only as this authority is clothed with tenderness does it become other than cruelty.

A democratic government legislates the will of the majority for the common welfare, and imposes its laws upon the minority; but in the relationship between husband and wife or between friends, any attempt to dictate is fatal. There must be mutual understanding and co-operation rather than discipline. The one who undertakes to *make the other over* after his own desires is riding for a fall. Whether this discipline goes under the name of "wife-whipping," "rolling-pin authority," or "nagging," the results are the same. Such an attitude does not deserve to be called love, but rather is a misplaced self-love.

In the relationship between a government and its people, and surely between friends or marriage partners, more progress can be made by developing mutual understanding and co-operation than by brute force. In the case of threatened anarchy, brute force may be required, but after the struggle is ended, it is the pathway of patient love that brings progress in human relations.[8] In the case of extreme cruelty, a marriage may break up. When and if it is saved, it is always through the discovery of agape love.

John Wesley must have had a glint of humor in his eyes as he wrote in his journal about one of his Methodists who told him he beat his wife regularly to improve her manners and felt that he enjoyed the blessing of God every time he did it! Though Mr. Wesley did not say it in so many words, he implied that this dominating husband knew little or nothing about either love for God or love for his wife!

Does your love help you to know when criticism and firm discipline are necessary, and how to give them without doing more harm than good? John Steinbeck describes such love in one of the pioneer mothers in his story of the early days in California:

Rama had ways of making her field: cooking, sewing, the bearing of children, housecleaning, seem the most important things in the world. . . . The children adored Rama when they had been good, for she knew how to stroke the tender places in the soul. Her praise could

---

[8] See Chap. VII, "Finding Peace and Fortitude Through Love."

be as delicate and sharp as her punishment was terrible. She automatically took charge of all children who came near her. Burton's two children recognized her authority as far more legally constituted than the changeable rules their own soft mother made, for the laws of Rama never changed, bad was bad and bad was punished, and good was eternally, delightfully good. It was delicious to be good in Rama's house! [9]

Such tenderness is truly the indispensable emotion. "There is no sound we are privileged to hear that is more spontaneous and uncorrupted than the laughter of tenderness: a kind of spilling over of delighted amusement at life—at the newness of it, the wonder, and the awkwardness of it." Such tender kindness enables one of mature strength and experience to do two essential things: ". . . to cherish a young one as dear and valuable at each stage of growth; and to nurture him, so that he is gradually prepared in body, habit system, and outlook for a future he himself cannot prevision." [10]

Thank God, I had such a mother who cherished my brother and sisters and me even when we were wrong, but whose strong love did not overlook or cancel our wrongs until we faced them and made amends. She disciplined us, sometimes by an old-fashioned method; but she did it with a deep kindness that melted our hostilities. She knew how to stroke the tender places in my soul. "It was delicious to be good" in my mother's presence!

Such tenderness is as indispensable in marriage, in community or national life, as it is in parent-child or friend-to-friend relationships. The ability to stand for what one believes is right and best with a tender kindness enables us to help rather than curse those with whom we are associated.

II. Giving-Love Goes Beyond Sentimentality

Strong love is not merely tenderness. Tenderness itself bogs down when it degenerates into sentimentality. Now sentiment is a beau-

[9] *To a God Unknown*, pp. 37-38. Used by permission of Viking Press, Inc.

[10] Harry and Bonaro Overstreet, *The Mind Alive* (New York: W. W. Norton & Co., 1954), p. 297.

51

tiful thing in a home or in any other place; but "the value of a sentiment is the amount of sacrifice you are prepared to make for it." [11] The trouble with what we may call sentimental love is that we are too often interested in letting others make the sacrifice. In the name of love there is often cruelty when we are more concerned with how *we feel* than with the highest good of those we love. Love is strong and kind only when it seeks for others the highest good—God's will—and not our own sentimental picture of that good. "Love is the active concern for the life and the growth of that which we love." [12]

The beautiful Hymn to Love in I Cor. 13 declares pointedly that some people are willing to give up their bodies to be burned and all their goods to feed the poor, but still it profits them nothing. Why? Because they do not really love others. They do not care about the poor. They are interested first in proving their own goodness or superiority.

This is the evil of much that is called love: we do not really desire the good for others as much as we wish to exalt and preserve our sentimental image of ourselves. For instance, there was the idealistic college student who went to the Near East as a missionary only to give up in disillusionment when he found he did not really possess the spirit he taught. Explaining his failure he wrote, "The boys saw through our shell. The idea had got around that when we teachers talked about love, it was not Christian love for the natives at all, but love for our own ideal of love!" [13]

There are far too many parents who love in this sentimental fashion, trying to live out their lives in the lives of their children, trying to make the children succeed where they have succeeded, or where they have failed but longed to succeed. Here is a boy with better than average intelligence who is bogged down in mathe-

[11] John Galsworthy.
[12] Eric Fromm, *The Art of Loving* (New York: Harper & Bros., 1956), p. 26.
[13] Rollo May, *Springs of Creative Living* (Nashville: Abingdon-Cokesbury Press, 1940), p. 47.

matics. He can't do even the most elementary addition or subtraction. His father is a brilliant accountant who loves his math and expects his son to maintain the family name. The boy, in trying to protect his freedom to be himself, transfers his antagonism from his dad to his arithmetic. His father was "pushing too hard," explained the doctor to whom they went for help. His father's efforts to help were not out of a concern for his son, but rather out of sentimental concern for the image of himself he wanted his son to fulfill!

The blockade of sentimental love prevents many parents from succeeding in their attempts to transfer their moral ideals to their children. They really love their moral or social standards, including a rigid family pride, more than their children—though they would be indignant if anyone accused them of it. They are like the pious, sentimental mother Matilda in William Law's description who insists that her daughters read their books of devotion, but whose daughters are afraid to meet her if they have missed church and still more afraid if they are not laced as strait as they can possibly be. We do not wonder that the eldest daughter dies at the age of twenty, having lived as long as she could under this discipline, and that the youngest daughter runs away with a handsome gambler. "Matilda says, she should die with grief . . . , but that her conscience tells her, she has contributed nothing to it herself." [14] She points out all she has done to see that her children are brought up piously in good morals. In countless modern homes the tragedy is repeated: loving their moral standing more than their children, parents find their children rebelling at the moralizing and doing the opposite.

The parents whose moral teachings are most likely to be observed are those who have built up a companionship with their children—a rapport in which the children have learned to see for themselves what is right and wrong about certain acts and to make their own decisions in the light of their understandings. Families

[14] From *A Serious Call to a Devout and Holy Life*, by William Law, ed. John W. Meister, *et al.* (Philadelphia: Westminster Press, 1955), pp. 122-23.

that have fun together, play and work together, and pray together are much more likely to have a strong moral consciousness than those where parents simply "read the riot act." The parents who have the confidence of their children, so that together they may face the moral problems that confront them, will be able to help their children choose the best.[15]

Certainly moral ideals must be taught; no kind of real goodness can be forced. It must come from the inside, caught from wholesome faith and love in which morality is attractive. Carlyle's words concerning his mother describe the reason her moral and religious influence was so effective:

My kind mother did me one altogether invaluable service. She taught me, less indeed by word than by act and daily reverent habitude, her own simple version of the Christian faith. . . . The highest whom I knew on earth I saw bowed down with awe unspeakable, before a Higher One in Heaven. Such things, especially in infancy, reach inward to the very core of your being.

Giving-love "seeketh not her own"—that is, does not demand "for *my* sake" the fulfillment of my own desires in others even if these desires are good and proper. In the words of Carl Sandburg, you must be big enough to "loosen your hands, let go and say goodby!" Only thus will those we love ever respect and appreciate our teachings and in the long run come back to us free and whole. Every parent, every husband and wife, every friend, needs to possess the spirit of Mrs. Ramsay MacDonald who, according to her husband's memoirs, regarded her own children as "treasures given to her to guard and protect, not to thrust and mold into a mere image of herself!" There is a world of difference between guarding and helping and thrusting and molding!

[15] See Chap. VII, "Finding Peace and Fortitude Through Love," for a fuller development of this question.

III. Giving-Love Sets the Loved One Free

Giving Christlike love always sets free those who are loved; but acquisitive, possessive love leads us to use every wile we know, either through exaggerated kindness or domineering harshness, to thrust and mold those we love and keep them just the way we want them.

This is the tragedy of the possessive mate as dramatized in Joseph Kramm's play *The Shrike*. Jim Downs finds himself in the psychiatric ward of the city hospital after having taken 156 phenobarbital tablets. His brother warns him that his wife, the only one who can secure his release, will not co-operate unless she knows definitely that he will come back to her on her terms:

HARRY: "She loves you, Jim. She wants you back. She told the doctor that. I won't try to explain it. I think there's something distorted in taking advantage of your being here to get you back this way. But I don't question that she loves you—and my advice to you is to be in love with her. That's the only way you'll get out of here quickly." [16]

Such love is a tragic evil. "There is no question that she loves you," but her love is the "I-love-*you*-but-want-you-to-serve-*me*" kind that enslaves rather than frees.

Wise love must learn the difference between helping and meddling. Dr. Darrell, in O'Neil's *Strange Interlude,* has used his friend Nina to satisfy his own selfish love, even though she remains married to another man. Their excuse is that her husband is unable to give her a child. So the doctor, under the pretext of scientific objectivity, enters into a relationship that is purely acquisitive and selfish. Nina has a child by the doctor and the child, Gordon, grows up to be warped and twisted by the lack of genuine love in his home. Too late, Nina appeals to Darrell to do something to change Gordon. Darrell answers: "I swore I'd never again meddle

[16] Act 3, scene 1, p. 164. Published by Random House and used by permission of the author.

with human lives, Nina! . . . You've got to give up owning people, meddling in their lives as if you were God and had created them!"

The irresponsibility of the doctor is inexcusable. But he does realize that to step in and attempt to force a change that only months of wise love could have made would be merely meddling. It is a crime to "meddle" in others' lives. Only giving-love can "help."

Nina answers with the desperate words that reveal her complete misunderstanding of real love: "I don't know what you mean, Ned. Gordon is my son, isn't he?" [17]

Like Nina, it is our inability to understand that we do not really *own* another that makes our loving so futile and hurtful. He is not *my* son. She is not *my* wife. He is not *my* husband. And *I* am not God. It is only as I respect you as a free person, of infinite value in your own right and not just for what you can do for my feelings, that I may be able to help you at all. All self-centered, acquisitive loving is meddling!

Since freedom is so necessary for growth, no wonder we fight so bitterly the encroachments of a nagging wife or husband, or a possessive parent or friend. Back of so many persons' inability to love is the ingrained defense against possessive love, a reaction that has carried over from childhood and become habitual. We look at others, even those we love, with miserable, suspicious eyes, because we were once enslaved by someone who "loved" us.

The only real antidote for the poisonous love that enslaves is the love that sets us free—the love that comes to both of us as we give our hearts to the Highest. Kahlil Gibran describes the kind of unity in marriage that gives freedom. It is a freedom in the love that keeps "spaces in your togetherness" so that your personalities are released rather than smothered, in which love is not a bond but rather "a moving sea between the shores of your souls." When you give your hearts "into each other's keeping," love is a bondage.

[17] Copyright, 1928, and used by permission of Random House, Inc.

When "only the hand of Life" contains your hearts, you are free! A commitment to love God with all your hearts results in the ability to love each other wisely and well.

Liberty in Love

Giving-love sets our loved ones free. It does so in the same way God seeks to set us free. "In this is love, not that we loved God but that he loved us and sent his Son" for us! (I John 4:10.)

Why does God love us? Not because we are worthy or have proved our lovableness or in any way merit his love. No, we may even have been enemies of God: "While we were yet helpless, at the right time Christ died for the ungodly. . . . God shows his love for us in that while we were yet sinners Christ died for us." (Rom. 5:6-8.)

This is the breath-taking assurance of those who share vitally in the Christian faith. Paul could not get over it. Had he not been a persecutor of Christ? And yet in his own experience he had met the love and forgiveness of Christ! His whole life therefore was a paean of amazed thanksgiving: "I who am the chief of sinners—to me is this grace given!"

Like Paul, those who learn to accept the security of Divine Love are more and more able to love intelligently, positively, with tenderness and strength. This is one of life's most hopeful facts.

God's love is revealed to us in many ways: through a strong mother or father love, or the love of a companion or friend, and supremely in the love of Christ which passeth all knowledge.

Not all mothers and fathers have shown this unmotivated, unconditional love. In fact, the father in the story of the prodigal son, in accepting his son back into the home after he had wasted his substance in riotous living in the far country, did not treat the boy in the way fathers usually treat prodigal sons. But Jesus told the story to say that even though most fathers would have rejected

57

their sons' penitence, this is the way God treats us! The fact that most of us know fathers with this kind of unconditional love is a great testimony to the effectiveness not only of Christ's teaching, but of his revelation in life of God's agape. The disciples saw his love and forgiveness and exclaimed, "He loved us and gave himself for us." This is the way God loves us—freely, spontaneously, unconditionally—not because we are worthy, but because his nature is love and because in his wisdom he is able to create within us the ability to love even as we are loved! "Beloved, if God so loved us, we also ought to love one another." (I John 4:11.)

God himself does not attempt to force goodness. "I have set before you life and death, blessing and curse; therefore choose life, that you and your descendants may live, loving the Lord your God, obeying his voice, and cleaving to him." (Deut. 30:19-20.) These words are the foreshadowing of the same amazing offer in the life of Jesus, whose cross was the result of man's misuse of freedom. "In this the love of God was made manifest among us, that God sent his only Son into the world, so that we might live through him!" (I John 4:9.)

Such Love-Divine is so great it makes us catch our breath and wait in reverence for its meaning: *God values the free, independent personality of his children so much that he sets us free—free even to choose the wrong and suffer for it and to bring indescribable suffering upon others as well.* But God does not leave us alone. There is a moral order which is inexorable: when we go against our true nature, we suffer; when we fulfill our true nature, we live! God does not spoon-feed his favorites or cancel the penalty of their mistakes; but his "tender-kindness" comes to us even in the suffering of our wrong choices. In the suffering of the man on the cross, millions of love-starved, defeated, rejected children see the strong love of God the Father and find the power for strong love through him. His is the love that will not let me go—not forcing, not compelling, not nagging or threatening, but leading tenderly, patiently, in the gentle persuasion of an Eternal Kindness!

"We love him, because he first loved us." This is the order of maturity—the strong, kind love that endures all things, believes all things, hopes all things! Such love never fails.

Then it is that many, many times because I give love, I am loved; but my loving is not dependent upon my being loved. Sometimes, indeed, we are hated by those to whom we give our love, as Jesus was. The fact that I love does not guarantee that I will be loved. If it did, it would cease to be love and become mere prudence. Nevertheless, the blessed experience of receiving love is made more likely and rewarding by my giving love. But I *must not* give love *in order* that I may be loved. To do so is to miss the most blessed and divinely inspired opportunities of life.

"[Love]," wrote Emerson, "is a fire that kindling its first embers in the narrow nook of a private bosom, caught from a wandering spark out of another private heart, glows and enlarges until it warms and beams upon multitudes of men and women, upon the universal heart of all, and so lights up the whole world and all nature with its generous flames!"

> "All I can do is love you,"
> She said in my distress,
> As if it were but little,
> And she were doing less
> Than others might. But loving—
> By all the tears that fall—
> Is the most that anyone can do
> For anyone at all.[18]

Yes, strong, wise, giving-love is the most that anyone can do for anyone at all! How strong and outgoing is your love?

---

[18] Jane Merchant, "By All the Tears." Used by permission of *National Parent-Teacher* and the author.

IV. Learning to Love Generously

"He that provideth not for his own household is worse than an infidel!" The "old man," as his sons called him, was justifying his stinginess by quoting a Bible proverb. All their lives he had driven himself and them and their poor bedraggled mother by the whip of some threatened insecurity. But as their bank account increased and their lands multiplied, so did his feelings of insecurity. His sons cursed him, hated him even as they worked for him. Now they rebelled openly.

"You do not love us," they shouted at him. "You love your wealth, not us!" Like so many of the rest of us, this man had treated persons as things, and things as he should have treated persons. Now he realized he had lost something far more valuable than all his riches.

A sinister mistake indeed! And yet one that is committed in some degree by everyone who has not learned to let genuine love handle his anxieties and insecurities.

Thrift and prudence are both normal attitudes, part of a healthy drive for self-preservation; yet like any other virtues, without genuine giving-love they degenerate into a hideous miserliness and a self-saving prudence that become self-destroying and at the same time rob others of the creative blessings we could give them.

Love is ever giving and forgiving. It cannot be given overprudently, calculatingly, but freely, lavishly, extravagantly; for this is the nature of strong love which we may share with God. God gives beauty and life to all things. For every seed that sprouts and grows there are millions that seem to be wasted. For every flower that is admired by human eyes there are billions that bloom unseen. For every star visible to our delighted vision, there are billions more moving in their stately galaxies that cannot be seen even through the most powerful telescope. What blessed prodigality is revealed everywhere in creation!

The greatest giving known to human ken is that which we celebrate at Christmas. We call it the Incarnation: God giving himself in a little bundle of human flesh wrapped in swaddling clothes in a manger—and all this *for us!* "In this the love of God was made manifest among us, that God sent his only Son into the world, so that we might live through him." (I John 4:9).

Few of us would question the wise spendthriftness with which God endows us with life and love; and yet this kind of generous giving love is difficult indeed for us to see and to make a part of our lives.

For from the time of Plato, through Augustine and other Christian moralists, down to our own times, every worthy father in any land or age has wisely counseled his sons and daughters in the spirit if not the words of the Old Testament proverb:

> Go to the ant, O sluggard;
>   consider her ways, and be wise
> Without having any chief,
>   officer or ruler,
> she prepares her food in summer,
>   and gathers her sustenance in harvest.
> How long will you lie there, O sluggard?
> A little sleep, a little slumber,
>   a little folding of the hands to rest,
> and poverty will come upon you like a vagabond!
>
> —Prov. 6:6-11

Prudence, therefore, is a "practical wisdom . . . the ability to regulate and discipline oneself through the exercise of the reason; skill or sagacity in the management of . . . business affairs; provident use of resources" (Webster's International Dictionary). Thrift is similar to prudence, meaning the employment of good husbandry and economic management.

Surely these virtues are needed in our day, when men are tempted to emphasize security by big government or big corporations or big labor unions at the expense of individual responsibility and freedom. The value of government or business or labor in helping to provide for the material well-being of its constituents is indisputable. But when security is considered more desirable than personal responsibility and freedom, laziness is encouraged, totalitarian governments are made possible, and deeper spiritual values are lost. This is to say that prudence and thrift in their normal rightful place are indeed necessary and are expressions of loving concern.

Blessed Spendthriftness

Nevertheless, there is a kind of spendthriftness that is truly blessed, a prodigality of extravagance and lavishness in giving which is of the very essence of the good life at its fullest and best. The blessings of humanity today have come not only through the lavish gifts of God, but in the uncalculating prodigality of the labors and lives of our Pasteurs and Lincolns, our Socrateses, Livingstones, and Schweitzers and, supremely, of our Christ, "who gave himself a ransom for all." As William Blake says it so accurately, "There are times when the road of excess leads to the palace of wisdom." Surely a love that is purely judicious is always to be questioned. Love, by its very nature, goes beyond the nicely calculated less and more.

Here, then, is our dilemma: how can we be wisely prudent and at the same time give lavishly out of a generous love? Jesus described our problem and the way out in the great paradox:

Whoever would save his life will lose it; and whoever loses his life for my sake and the gospel's will save it. For what does it profit a man, to gain the whole world and forfeit his life? . . . Give, and it will be given to you; good measure, pressed down, shaken together, running over. . . . Whoever would be first among you must be slave of all. (Mark 8:35-36; Luke 6:38; Mark 10:44.)

These paradoxes have always been considered folly to the worldly wise who in all their giving are primarily concerned with getting, but in the long run they are descriptions of the deepest law of human life.

The most revealing illustration in the records of Jesus of the love that is beautifully extravagant and yet wisely prudent is found in the story of his experience with the woman with the alabaster box of precious ointment. The woman, whom we shall call Mary, came to a banquet given to Jesus by Simon the Pharisee. We do not know much about her except that she loved her Lord greatly, not in a sensual way, but for what he was. She believed him to be the Messiah, the one sent of God to bring hope and salvation to her and her people and to all mankind, and therefore worthy of her highest devotion. Before the amazed eyes of the disciples and the other guests, she broke the box of precious ointment, representing a value of at least three hundred denarii, or a year's wages (about three hundred dollars), and anointed him as one would anoint a king for his coronation. When Jesus did not rebuke her, the disciples, led by Judas, began to grumble: "Why this silly waste? How imprudent, unthrifty! This ointment might have been sold for a large sum and the money given to the poor."

And so it could. Who was right—the prudent Judas or the extravagant Mary? Jesus decided with Mary rather than with Judas. "Let her alone," he cried; "she has done a beautiful thing; without realizing it, she has anointed my body for the burial. . . . Wherever this gospel is preached in the whole world, this shall be told in memory of her." And so it has been. But Judas? Shortly thereafter he was holding out his hand and saying, "How much will you *give* me?" A few days later Jesus was heard to say of this prudent man, "It would have been better for that man if he had not been born!" And, ironically, the Gospel of John records (17:13), speaking of

63

the disciples, "None of them is lost but the son of [waste]!" His calculating prudence was the most foolish waste! Mary's lavish giving was the wisest prudence after all—a blessed extravagance and a glorious spendthriftness!

It is obvious that cautious thrift and calculating prudence may cause us to lose much more than that which we so carefully save. To obey the old Gesta Romanorum, "whatever you do, do cautiously and look to the end," often results in overlooking the opportunities that in the end are seen to be most valuable.

When is prudence wasteful folly and when is lavish giving a blessed act that makes life worth while? There is no rule of thumb here, just as there is also none in any of the other questions concerning good and evil. In each case the spirit of understanding love and the willingness to do the highest good—God's will—must be the deciding factor. Nevertheless, there are some clear-cut conclusions from observation and experience to guide our choice as we apply the spirit of Christlike love to each situation.

Generous Love Overcomes Insecurity

Generous love does not need to hide its feelings of insecurity behind an accumulation of material things and pleasures. It is our fear of insecurity that makes us unable to use our physical and material resources generously and productively.

Insecurity is the natural state of all human life. "We have this treasure in earthen vessels," declared Paul, "to show that the transcendent power belongs to God and not to us." (II Cor. 4:7.) What we do with our insecurity determines our blessedness or our misery. Do we anxiously seek to remove it in our own way or do we accept it and make the most of it while we rest in the deeper security of the love of God? Sin and evil too often have their root in our pitiful attempts to make ourselves secure in our own right apart from God's good will for us.

To illustrate: What is jealousy but miserliness, the grasping attempt to be secure in love? And what are lust and gluttony but miserliness, the search for security through sensualism! Avarice and envy and covetousness are nothing but miserliness, the striving for security through the possession of things. We do live in an uncertain world, where we have only a few minutes to live, so to speak; this is part of the nature of human existence. But the way out of insecurity is not through the cautious saving of our physical, mental, and material possessions and powers. Such miserliness in life means literally misery and wretchedness!

Here is a man who slaves fourteen, sixteen, eighteen hours a day to make a success, to get ahead. Why? Not because he or his family really need so much; but because he is basically insecure and is miserably trying to cover up and escape from his insecurity.

Misers of Joy

Remember, there are misers of pleasure and joy, of strength and love, as well as of gold! Some of us who are young, and some not so young, are hoarding our times of pleasure and joy until the wee hours of the morning. Why? Surely not because we are really enjoying ourselves. Where will you find a more joyless group than one trying desperately to have fun at three o'clock in the morning? Why then? Because we are misers of joy, trying to accumulate and hoard our hours of joy and pleasure "before we are too old," afraid there is something of joy that we will miss.

Here is a person who never marries, not because he is consumed by some great mission that makes married life unwise—but because he has what he calls "foresight." He is cautious, he says; he has seen too much suffering in others who are married, and he is not going to make the same mistake. He is too prudent to fall in love because he is insecure and afraid he will lose what little security and independence he has. He is like Steve Canyon, in Milton Caniff's comic strip, fleeing from a woman who loved him. Steve, a handsome lieutenant colonel in the air force, seems to have this problem frequently; and this time he disposes of it with the words:

"I had better stick to tin birds. If you just feed them, they won't let you down."

Steve Canyon seems somehow typical of all insecure men and women who remain *prudently* single, or who refuse to bear children or take any creative responsibility in a community of love. They miss some of the deepest joys of life which come only to those who are able to give themselves to another in unselfish love. This is not to say that there are not some single persons who have found, as many priests and celibate Christians have found through the years, abundant love in the giving of themselves to meet the needs of others; but it is to say that marriage and home, with all the lavish cost, is a blessed spendthriftness to those who know the spirit of Christlike love.

Yes, it surely costs to love. You really stick your neck out, as the old saying goes, when you get married and have children. You stick your neck out when you become close friends. And to accept discipleship as a follower of Christ is foolhardy indeed. There is the shadow of a cross, not only on the manger of Bethlehem but on every mother and her child. There are long, weary hours of watching beside a sickbed. There are days of anxious concern as the youth learns to stretch his wings and discovers the price of freedom. There are years of hard work and self-denial when there is love in a world like this.

But there is a wisdom in the self-sacrifice of love that puts to shame all "purely dutiful philanthropy." The beautiful story by O. Henry called "The Gift of the Magi" is a modern counterpart of the woman with the alabaster box. It is the touching story of a young husband and wife who were poverty-stricken in everything except love. When Christmas came they had no money with which to buy a present for each other that could in any way express their affection. Jim thought of the gold watch which had been passed down to him from his father and grandfather and remembered Della's lovely braids of brown hair. So he went out and sold the watch in order to buy a set of jeweled combs which Della had wanted so

66

long. And Della, remembering how Jim valued his gold watch, went out and sold her hair and bought a platinum fob and chain for his watch! The story will live because it describes in an unforgettable way the sacrificial devotion that makes love "the greatest thing in the world."

When there is love, there is a cross sooner or later. But the wisdom of the cross is greater than the wisdom of the world. The wisdom of the worldly-wise is foolishness when all the chips are in. Who can estimate the glory in love returned as mother and dad see the child grown to maturity, graduating from college, building a worthy place in life! Or who can describe the glory in the soul of the servant of humanity who at great cost has developed a cure for yellow fever or polio, or has helped stem the tide of evil in a home, a community, or a nation!

Edward Young accurately describes in his "Night Thoughts" the experience of millions who prudently seek to save their lives and end up by losing them:

> At *thirty* man *suspects* himself a Fool;
> *Knows* it at *Forty*, and reforms his Plan;
> At *fifty* chides his infamous Delay,
> Pushes his prudent Purpose to *Resolve*;
> In all the Magnanimity of Thought
> Resolves; and re-resolves; then dies the same!

Be miserly with yourself and your possessions, and you will be wretchedly miserable. How pitifully tragic it is that so many of us are "saving up" our health, our wealth, our energies, because there are many things we need and want and we are afraid we will run short, especially as time runs out. So we go skimping, calculating, planning—breathlessly anxious lest we fail to get all we want.

When You Suspect Yourself a Fool!

How silly it all appears when we stop to look at it! As a woman who was dying with cancer said to her pastor: "You know, Reverend, lying here waiting to die has some good points. I've been thinking. It's all so silly. . . . I mean life . . . its arguments, feuds, and all. . . . Sometimes I feel like laughing at life. When I think of the heart-aches and tears and . . . worries [here she smiles], I just feel like laughing. It's all so futile! . . . Isn't it in the Bible, 'Vanity, vanity, all is vanity'?" She was thinking of the folly of her overprudent life with its useless worries! What vanity indeed!

If only you and I might have some better perspective before we get to the place where we can't really do anything about it! Instead of losing our lives in anxious striving over the things that really do not matter, we could learn to give ourselves in the places where it counts the most and let God give us the kingdom of heaven, which in the long run includes the things we really want.

This is the only lasting, dependable security on earth: trust in the God of love who is so amazingly dependable he never lets you down. To give oneself fully, joyously, and completely to the highest is indeed the wisest prudence of which man is capable. "Be grateful," says the author of Hebrews, "for receiving a kingdom that cannot be shaken, and thus let us offer to God acceptable worship, with reverence and awe." (12:28.)

Generous Love Gives a Wiser Choice of Values

Generous love refuses to countenance or preserve and exalt a twisted sense of values. The saving of persons is always more important to love than the saving of things; and the door to hope and life, for others as well as ourselves, is more important than the saving of a few more dollars in a false quest for security. Shall I try to hoard myself and my possessions only to find, in the end, my possessions worthless and my life lost in wretchedness and disgust? Or shall I spend wisely of myself and give of my possessions gladly in the greatest cause on earth, to find in the end all those rich and rewarding treasures that last forever? These, declared Jesus, are the alternatives facing each of us: "Whoever would save his life will lose it; and whoever loses [gives] his life for my sake and the gospel's will save it" (Mark 8:35).

> Love that is hoarded, moulds at last
> Until we know some day
> The only thing we ever have
> Is what we give away.
>
> . . . . . .
>
> It is the things we always hold
> That we will lose some day;
> The only things we ever keep
> Are what we give away.[1]

Waste or wisdom? Take your choice!

Judas said, "Waste!" Jesus said, "A beautiful thing that will last forever." Time and the experience of history say that Jesus was right. Look at the waste of a misspent life squandered on false values, whether hanging by a rope over a cliff outside Jerusalem or hanging by a rope of petty, inconsequential nothings over a cliff of misery and failure. While Mary's beautiful, outgoing love is written into the record of history along with the other great givers whose blessed spendthriftness have enriched the life of mankind, Judas is hanged by his own miserly prudence.

Prudence and thrift are virtues only as we are careful and cautious about the right things. James Russell Lowell puts these words into his "Pious Editor's Creed":

> It aint by princerples nor men
> My preudunt course is steadied,—
> I scent which pays the best, an' then
> Go into it baldheaded!

Prudence is always wrong as calculating foresight that makes profit more important than principles or the people involved.

---

[1] Louis Ginsberg, "Song," from *The Everlasting Minute*, published by Liveright Co. Used by permission of the author.

Beauty and love, kindness and charity, worship and self-giving—
are not waste but indeed the highest wisdom!

The mother of a little eight-year-old boy was sick and in the hospital. He had been running errands and saving up his nickels and dimes for several weeks. When he had five dollars, he went to the florist and picked out the prettiest red roses he could find and brought them to his mother. Was this waste or wisdom? Ask his mother! Ask the boy grown up fifty years later!

What would our world be without such prodigal waste—if you still insist on calling it waste?

What would it be without such men as John Wesley, who rode eighty thousand miles on horseback through rain and storm, who preached sometimes as many as five sermons in a day, who made thousands of pounds by his writings and poured it all back into his work? His motto was, "Make all you can; save all you can; give all you can." And he knew that unless you kept this last part of the motto, the rest would be imprudent prudence—folly.

Or Francis Asbury, the Prophet of the Long Road, who never married, and who suffered great pain and misery because he had spent so many hours riding through the mountains and swamplands of the New World; but who in his life spread the spiritual awakening of Methodism through all of early America.

Or St. Francis de Sales, the spiritual guide of seventeenth-century France, who when reproached by a friend for the reckless extravagance in which he was giving himself, replied, "It is not necessary that I should live, but it is necessary that God's work should go on."

Or Dick Sheppard, whose ministry to the people at St. Martin's-in-the-Fields in London was so prodigal in the spending of his energy that his doctor reproved him sharply: "Why do you give yourself to every sick and suffering person you meet? Why sit up all night with a sick boy?" At Sheppard's reply that he thought it would help and comfort the lad, and besides he had promised he would, the doctor also said, "What a waste!"

Is such generous love a prodigal waste? Well, it depends on your definition of values. Was it waste when Frank Laubach, after spending the best years of his life as a missionary to the Moros on the island of Mindanao in the Philippines, gave himself to share with the peoples of the world his discovery of a quick way to teach illiterate people to read and to write? Ask one woman in Yucatan, Mexico, whom he had taught to read. When he saw her progress, he said, "You have learned so quickly, you would make a good teacher." She stretched out her arms and burst out crying: "I don't understand why you came down here to teach a nobody like me, I'm nobody. What do you want?"

"I don't want anything," answered Laubach. "I learned this from Jesus. He spent every minute of his days helping people. He just walked down the road looking from right to left. If the people he met were hungry, he fed them; if they were sick, he healed them; and when they were blind, he opened their yes. You are blind and that's the reason your people are hungry here and in debt; but Jesus opened your eyes and you'll never be that way again!"

Gratefully she looked up with a smile through her tears and answered, "I'll teach others!"

Ask the prisoner in an Indian jail who was a poet and who was singing his thanks to Laubach as he visited these several hundred prisoners who had been taught to read. They had used his method, each one who was taught teaching another. Now they were in the aisles of the prison to welcome him. The warden interpreted as the prisoner poet sang:

> My soul is singing, it has been set free!
> My body was free before I came to this prison
> But my soul was imprisoned.
> Now my body is in prison
> But my soul is soaring toward heaven!
> Who am I that I dare dream the unutterable dreams?
> Hopes for myself, for my children, and my country
> Now flood my soul!

71

"The face of that prisoner was like an angel," says Laubach as he describes the experience. "The warden and I wept unashamed, side by side. For them I was their saviour out of death and hell and oppression. Literacy was breaking that chain of despair and my soul was singing too!" [2]

Lavish loving! If the development of the best that is in mankind is the highest value, if peace on earth is desirable, this noble, self-giving love of Laubach and of those who follow in the spirit of Christ is the greatest wisdom on earth!

How Do You Know It Is Worth the Cost?

It all depends on the value of things. Of course you can't prove by any sort of scientific means that it is better to bear poverty for the sake of truth than to grow rich through lies. Nor can you prove that Beethoven's "Moonlight Sonata," or Raphael's "Madonna and Child," or the Taj Mahal is beautiful, nor that it is better to give oneself and one's possessions for the freeing and ennobling of mankind. Nevertheless, there are some things which the experience of mankind declares with great unanimity. One of these experiences testifies to the conviction of many thousands that in Jesus Christ there is a revelation of the self-giving love of God which is the deepest reality of our universe. "Love is the Greatest Thing in the World," wrote Henry Drummond. Because of God's love for all the world of human lives, there is something in the lowliest and the least that is worth living, worth saving, worth suffering and dying for!

True, to our prosaic age in which materialistic and financial measuring sticks have been applied to everything, the only prudent thing is to save what you have. The scientific mind is trained to think of nothing as beautiful or ugly, good or bad, but "everything is, or at least may be, interesting."

[2] These stories taken from a tape recording of an address by Frank Laubach at Koronis, Camp Furthest Out, Paynesville, Minnesota, August, 1956.

Willam H. Roberts puts the inadequacy of scientific materialism thus:

"If you want to kill a quarter of a million, or more, men, women, and children in one terrific BANG," our scientists have told us, "we can supply atomic, hydrogen, or cobalt bombs, or other weapons less noisy but even more frightful." If we ask, "But *ought* we to kill so many human beings, either in one monstrous explosion or in many lesser ones?" the scientists [as scientists] cannot answer. The prevailing philosophy of science brusquely brushes off all questions of obligation or of value as "meaningless." The question actually seems a case of indecent exposure—as though a strip-tease performer were to interrupt the singing of a high mass by attempting to go through her act.[3]

Roberts shows how even science in its devotion to "certainty, exactness, universality, and system" depends on the "renunciation of all selfish ends or preferences and depends on the unproved values of lavish self-giving to a cause." But he warns:

A society that pays drivers of beer trucks more than teachers of children, that rates movie stars above astronomers and millionaires above those that are rich in thought, turns its values upside down. Sooner or later it is sure to suffer a fearful penalty. One item of that penalty will be the decline, even the disappearance of science.[4]

Here it needs to be said that a great many modern scientists are realizing the inadequacy of the old causal determinism that ignores the questions of "Why?" and "Whence?" They too are affirming the importance to mankind of the spiritual and moral values in religion which must work with science to develop the best in man. These scientists are also men and women of faith in the Unseen Love and Goodness at the Heart of All Things. They under-

[3] "A Shift of Accent," in *Religion and Life* (Autumn, 1956), p. 601.
[4] *Ibid.*, pp. 601-2.

stand with Lecomte du Noüy that "there exists a chasm between the world of quality and of quantity which science can never bridge."[5] For truly it is only the devotion and sacrifice of a mighty giving-love that can ever bridge the chasm between a world of unimaginable physical power and a world of moral and spiritual poverty and weakness.

We who have been willing to spend billions so prodigally on war must be willing to give just as lavishly, and infinitely more wisely, ourselves and our sons and daughters as well as our money in the cause of peace. The "give-away programs" of our government, as they are sometimes called, may not at times have been conducted in the wisest manner, partly because too much of the spirit behind them has not been right. It is true, as the enemies of the program say, that America can never *buy* its way into the good will and co-operation of other peoples in the cause of peace. But it is just as true that the genuine, positive contributions for peace will come from the heart of giving-love, which sees other people as loved by God and infinitely precious in his sight, and therefore worthy of respect and dignity. Such love will find ways to co-operate in the prevention of war and the building of lasting peace.[6]

One of the surest ways giving-love will take in our divided, suspicious world is in the local and world-wide ministries of the Church. For the Church, in spite of its faults and frailties, is the best expression of Christlike love available to man. Perhaps weakly, ineptly in some places, its work is done; but all over the world the beautiful extravagance of love is poured out in hospitals, in schools, and in the personal ministries of those who are controlled by the love of Christ (II Cor. 5:14).

Is it waste or wisdom to give proportionately of our time, talents, and money to the church and allied movements as they carry on a world-wide mission beginning with the children next door and the

[5] *Op. cit.*, p. 182.
[6] See Chap. VII, "Finding Peace and Fortitude Through Love."

wounded man across the street and extending to the farthest corner of the earth? There are many who say it is "pure waste."

What is waste and what is wisdom? In one year we in the United States of America spent $103 per capita for liquor; $2,700,000,000 for movies and recreation; $7,000,000,000 for jewelry, furs, and gambling; $10,000,000,000 for cosmetics (as we call our modern alabaster ointment); and the paltry sum of $900,000,000 for all churches and charities, or three cents per week per capita for benevolent giving. I am not against movies and recreation, or cosmetics and the beauty parlor; they have their places. But what about the imprudent prudence and miserly thrift of Christians who put cigarettes, movies, cosmetics, and recreation before the work of their Lord? Someone suggests that perhaps they might better pledge their loyalty to Coty perfumes, or Liggett and Myers tobacco, or Metro-Goldwyn-Mayer! Instead of a cross on the altar of their lives there should be placed a bottle of Chanel No. 5, a carton of Lucky Strikes, or a bundle of stocks and bonds. Christians today are giving less per capita according to our ability than we were during the depths of the depression, although we have twice as much!

Prudence and thrift are truly wise only when they are joined with a prodigal, lavish self-giving love to Him whose great love is our security and our hope, and the hope of our homes and of our world.

Here, then, is our choice: Are we going to be miserly, trying to get and keep for ourselves all the artificial security and pleasures we can get, until we lose ourselves and our civilization? Or are we going to spend ourselves and whatever we have, lovingly and thankfully, in the greatest cause on earth—the development of faith and character through which the gifts of science may be used to create and bless rather than curse and destroy? Generous giving-love? Is it waste or wisdom? Take your choice.

Our age is an age of moderate virtue
And of moderate vice
When men will not lay down the Cross
Because they will never assume it.
Yet nothing is impossible, nothing,
To men of faith and conviction.
Let us therefore make perfect our will.
O GOD, help us! [7]

These strong words of T. S. Eliot underline the tragedy and the hope of Christendom. Personal and social salvation depends on giving-love. This is the highest wisdom I know.

[7] From *The Rock* by T. S. Eliot, copyright, 1934, by Harcourt, Brace and Co., Inc. Used by permission of Harcourt, Brace and Co., Inc., and Faber and Faber, Ltd.

V. Love Making Duty Divine

> I slept and dreamed that life was beauty.
> I woke—and found that life was duty.[1]

So do we all. But whether our duty is delightful or depressing depends on whether or not we have an adequate store of strong, wise love from which to draw our resources.

I may accept the conclusions of the preceding chapters without question. I may decide that my purpose in life is to give love as generously and wisely as I know how. This goal may be defined in terms of "service" and "duty." But when I thus devote my life to high duty, I may be bitterly disappointed in the results. The frustrating paradox that baffles many well-intentioned souls is this: You and I may lose our lives even as we seek to save them in the fulfillment of duty!

For there is a deadening duty and an unholy service which, like twin demons, ride the weary, frustrated lives of a great many outwardly virtuous people.

"I must do my duty," we sometimes groan, as with gritted teeth we render our service.

Or else with hysterical enthusiasm we plunge into some "holy cause."

It is possible to sacrifice oneself for "honor" or to join a crusade for "justice" or "righteousness," and find the justice turning into injustice and the righteousness becoming unrighteousness with a vengeance! We may be part of the multitudes of *do-gooders* (and I do not use the word derisively), breathlessly rushing, pushing, sweating to help others; and then, too often, finding our help doing more harm than good, at least to ourselves.

[1] Ellen Sturgis Hooper, "Beauty and Duty."

Why such results? Because there is something sadly lacking in the love that motivates too many of our actions. "If I give away all I have, and if I deliver my body to be burned, but have not love, I gain nothing."(I Cor. 13:3.)

"The delusion of duty," writes one well-known doctor, is the one factor that "causes most of our suffering. . . . Nothing else causes so much neurosis, insanity and disease." [2]

I am not, of course, recommending a life of selfish unconcern or minimizing the value of duty and unselfish service.

> So nigh is grandeur to our dust,
>   So near is God to man,
> When Duty whispers low, *Thou must*,
>   The youth replies, *I can*.[3]

The progress of civilization depends not only on youth saying, "I can," but on some of us who are no longer young continuing to say it.

"He went about doing good" is the simple but eloquent way the Gospel describes Jesus' relationship with his fellow men. And so it is with any of the true helpers and servants of mankind.

My purpose, therefore, in this chapter is twofold:

1. To illustrate and emphasize the fact that only the love that is wise, strong, and outgoing in its unconditioned generosity can give to our good acts true perspective and worth; and that without such love our service becomes a drag, and our duty demonic.

2. To indicate the way in which "real" love makes our service truly blessed, and the doing of our duty deeply satisfying and rewarding to ourselves as well as to others.

There is such a way, and finding it results in the betterment of all, including my own ability to live joyously:

[2] David Seabury, *How Jesus Heals Our Minds Today* (Boston: Little, Brown and Co., 1941), p. 138.
[3] Ralph Waldo Emerson, "Voluntaries."

> The sweetest lives are those to duty wed,
> Whose deeds both great and small,
> Are close-knit strands of an unbroken thread,
> Where love ennobles all.[4]

One of the most beautiful scenes in the New Testament is the picture of Jesus in the Upper Room before his crucifixion, spending his last hour with his disciples.

> When Jesus knew that his hour had come to depart out of this world to the Father, having loved his own . . . he loved them to the end. . . . Jesus, knowing that the Father had given all things into his hands, and that he had come from God and was going to God, rose from supper, laid aside his garments, and girded himself with a towel. Then he poured water into a basin, and began to wash the disciples' feet.

There has been no service in history more rewarding than this tender act of strong love, the only basis upon which any service or duty is ever truly good.

Love Seeks No Escape Through Duty

Duty and service are always disappointing, even demonic, when I am attempting to use them as escapes from my own inner failure, or as attempts to punish myself. The French Foreign Legion is said to be made up largely of men disappointed in love or disgusted with life. So millions of defeated persons seek escape from themselves by joining some good movement or by assuming burdensome obligations in their homes, churches, and communities.

Surely, calling attention to this fact does not minimize the good services performed by the countless sincere persons in these various groups. There is a value in doing good in the very doing of it. Often persons who have done but very little for anyone other than themselves or their immediate families discover the joy of giving-love when they accept opportunities for service. Such persons

4 Attributed to Elizabeth Barrett Browning.

need to be encouraged in their new-found role of love. There is a very real sense in which Edwin Arnold's words are the description of all our human experience:

> The way to God is by the road of men;
> Find thy far heaven in near humanity;
> Love thy seen neighbor as thyself. Thereby
> Thou lovest Him Unseen, who is the All.

It is, however, dangerous and false to say to anyone that he can find God and a satisfying life *only* by serving man. He may find the devil instead and become bitter and cynical. Says Leslie Weatherhead, "Thousands of people in the churches are hiding from the relentless demands of Christ by doing His service." Whether the service of man leads me to God or to disgust is determined by the spirit with which I engage in the service.

A distinguished sociologist, after making a study of reformers and mass movements, writes: "A man is likely to mind his own business when it is worth minding. When it is not, he takes his mind off his own meaningless affairs by minding other people's business. . . . In running away from ourselves we either fall on our neighbor's shoulder or fly at his throat." [5]

Here is the origin of the gossips, meddlers, snoopers, viewers-with-alarm, the critical faultfinders, as well as some of the reformers. It is also the origin of the kind of "burden-bearers" whose assumption of heavy obligations in the home or community is tiring and exhausting, not only for them but for those whom they try to serve. Of course, it would be easy for any of us to point our finger at some people we know who are like this; but I suspect, if we are honest, there is not a single one of us who has not at times been a meddler, occasionally a gossip; and practically every one of us has assumed certain burdens for others which we resented and bore with painful dislike to ourselves and to them.

[5] Eric Hoffer, *The True Believer* (New York: Harper & Bros., 1951), p. 14.

Could it be true that in doing these things we are really running away from ourselves? Or at least that not loving our true selves enough we do not love these others? Not understanding the true cause of our discontent, as we look with miserable eyes on others we are likely to do one of two things: (1) Seek to make others miserable by overpowering them with all the good things we do for them, as if to say, "See how much I am doing for you. . . . I am sacrificing myself . . . you certainly ought to appreciate it!" Thus we make our victims so indebted that they feel they cannot draw a free breath. Or (2) we may seek to make them miserable by actually hurting them with vicious talk, carping criticism, or even "holy" persecution. Eager to believe the worst, we seek at times to find something in others which is bad and unworthy, and deserving of punishment, which we proceed to inflict. So we, too, either fall on our neighbor's shoulder or fly at his throat!

With their virtues they want to scratch out the eyes of their enemies; and they elevate themselves only that they may lower others. . . .
And many a one who cannot see men's loftiness, calleth it virtue to see their baseness far too well: thus calleth he his evil virtue.[6]

In this class belong the witch burners of every age, and the zealous reformers who gleefully pursue their reformations regardless of the suffering caused by their "justified cruelty"—in fact, the more suffering, the more gleeful they are! It was this as much as anything else that wrecked the prohibition movement, and which can impede the movement to remove racial injustice in America.

It is not easy to put ourselves in this class, and none of us is very likely to be there with conscious intent; but anytime you find yourself tempted to gossip, or to be thoughtlessly critical of those about you, or ardently to seek reforms that lead you to "well-justified" cruelty, you can know that you are fleeing "from your own

[6] Friedrich W. Nietzsche, *Thus Spake Zarathustra*, tr. Thomas Common (New York: The Modern Library, n.d.), pp. 101-2.

private ail"—you are sick on the inside. "The burning conviction that we have a holy duty toward others is often a way of attaching our drowning selves to a passing raft. What looks like giving a hand is often a holding on for dear life!" [7]

Could this be the reason the service you attempt is often so boring and deadening to you? Or that you find yourself fighting back at those who criticize and oppose you and who do not appreciate all you are doing for them? Does it proceed from a "miserable ailing spirit"? Is your duty to your family or your church a raft to which you cling because without it you would be drowned in misery? Could it be that with all your sincere conscious desire to serve, there is another and deeper compulsive need which may keep your service from being wise and loving? You may not confess it; but if it is so, you cannot perform your duty with the true perspective of what is good for you or those you love. Your service will never be deeply satisfying and rewarding, but rather out of it is likely to come the destructive hurtfulness of the "self-righteous."

My one suggestion at this point is that no one of us shrug it off by saying, "So-and-so is like that," and fail to be open to the need for a deeper orientation of our own spirits. It was this condition in the Pharisees which prompted Jesus to speak of the futility of "the blind leading the blind."

The drama *Susan and God,* by Rachel Crothers, portrays a rich, beautiful, intelligent woman always being driven by her duty to her club, her family, and to charitable causes. Now she has found "a new way to God" in "Lady Wiggam's movement." She throws herself passionately into the task of "changing others," confessing their sins for them, counseling with assurance, "God will help you." In the meantime her own daughter, Blossom, is lonesome and neglected in a private school and her husband, Barrie, is an alcoholic, partly at least because of her previous domineering attempts. In-

[7] Hoffer, *op. cit.,* p. 14.

stead of helping her friends, she causes bitter quarrels, breaks up one home, creates hostility and disgust instead of the attitudes of love she sought to bring.

Barrie overhears Susan talk about God's help: "No matter who you are—or what you do—you can be made over!" and he is deeply moved to say, "If you believe this, Susan, I believe it too. Do you mean He can do something about me, if I ask Him? If you do—I ask Him." [8] But even though he begins to conquer his bad habit through this new insight, Susan is more interested in her "movement" than in helping him. She is so wrapped up in her duty to God and others that she asks him for a divorce in order to devote herself more completely to her duty!

In the end Susan finds she is losing everything she really wants: her home, her daughter, her love, even God. She confesses the real motives which she had not realized before. As Barrie starts to leave her, she calls him back:

You don't know how rotten I've been. At first I hoped you would come home drunk—. . . and then when you didn't and didn't—I began to be awfully pleased with myself and think I was doing it. . . . I know my own stupidity has done all this to me. I know you are tired of my selfishness. Oh, I want to be so much more to you than I've been before.

The play ends with her prayer, "Oh, dear God, don't let me fall down again."

Her failure was the same as that of so many who enter "religious service" or dedicate themselves to some good cause. She found that everything she had been "gabbing about" was true concerning the transformations of life through faith in God, but that no matter how holy and right the message is, when the messenger lacks the spirit of Christlike love, the service is devastingly hurtful to all concerned.

This was at one time the trouble with John Wesley, who outdid all his friends in rigorous service to the sick and to those in prison, even as a missionary to the Indians in America. But becoming sick of heart and body, a failure at the age of thirty-five, he discovered that most of his good works were simply his desperate attempts to save himself. Then at Aldersgate, he made the great surrender of himself to the love of God in Christ, and found a new freedom and release that made strong love for others possible. From that hour, most of the things he did were creative and vital because his service was flowing out of the divine center of love for God and his fellows. His own explanation of what happened is significant: "I now live not as a slave, but as a son in my Father's house."

This same difficulty has been experienced by many of even the greatest Christians. When they were caught up in the joyous abandon of love for God, "knowing that they came from God and were going to God," their lives were remarkably fruitful. But when the self-saving, self-seeking, and self-protecting spirit was dominant, they were guilty of intolerance, bigotries, and cruelties that left dark shadows on their lives and movements.

Martin Luther was bitter toward his old friend and teacher Erasmus, who did not possess the vital faith as Luther saw it. There is nothing of the spirit of Christ in these words written about his opponent, "That venomous serpent, Erasmus, has once more been writing against me!" [9]

John Calvin had such bitter hatred toward Catellio, an old-time friend who had turned on him, that he not only "broke him in position, but permitted him to die in abject poverty, after accusing him of stealing driftwood on the Rhine." We have no room to criticize either of these great men. For no matter how exalted our duty or necessary our service, if it is done to save ourselves, there is no spirit of giving-love and it profits us nothing.

Contrast this with the giving-love of Christ, who washed the

[9] John Tulloch, *Martin Luther and Other Leading Reformers* (London: William Blackwood & Sons, 1933), p. 110. Used by permission.

feet of that little group of self-centered disciples, including Judas! What a scene that was! Jesus, kneeling before Judas who was to betray him, knowing his perfidy and disloyalty, yet Jesus, with tears in his eyes, lovingly, tenderly, washed the feet of Judas!

> Christ washed the feet of Judas!
> The dark and evil passions of his soul,
> His secret plot, and sordidness complete,
> His hate, his purposing, Christ knew the whole,
> And still in love he stooped and washed his feet.[10]

Duty and service are always demonic when through them I attempt to exalt and prove myself. If my devotion to a good cause is not due to the justice and worth of the cause but is an endeavor primarily to prove my own worth, and if the faith I embrace is largely to "bolster my confidence and legitimatize my success," my service is worthless to me and hurtful to others.

We must admit that much obedience to duty and sacrificial service is the result of a craving for recognition rather than of a love for others. "Vanity," said Napoleon, "made the revolution; liberty was only a pretext." How easy to recognize, among those who serve on the official board of a church or governing body of a P.T.A. or a service club, those who serve out of a genuine concern for the work being done and those who seek to lead, obstruct, shine, or whine out of vanity and ego! But how difficult to recognize these symptoms in our own acts!

There is the story of the society woman who wrote to a prominent social worker in New York, offering her services in his crusade to help the poor children of New York. She described her imperfections at length but concluded with the hope that her zeal for the cause would make up for her shortcomings. The social worker wrote this brief reply:

Dear Madam, Your truly magnificent shortcomings at present are too great. Nothing could prevent you from visiting them on victims of

[10] From "The Feet of Judas," by George Marion McClelland.

your humility. I advise that you love yourself more before you squander any love on others.[11]

How difficult for one who does not have enough love for himself to serve acceptably! In *The Rainbow*, D. H. Lawrence describes the character of Ursula, who was giving herself to first one service and then to another:

She was at this time a nuisance on the face of the earth. . . . She seemed to go with all her soul in her hands, yearning to the other person. Yet all the while, deep down at the bottom of her was a childish antagonism of distrust. She thought she loved everybody and believed in everybody, but because she could not love herself nor believe in herself, she mistrusted everybody with the mistrust of a serpent or a captured bird. . . . So she wrestled through her dark days of confusion, soulless, uncreated and unformed.[12]

You and I have been like that at times. Our service "soulless" because we have been unsure of our own worth, and our duty a handy tool with which we try to create and form something to prove our worth.

This is the tragedy of so much contemporary Christianity. No wonder a missionary, after years of experience, cried, "What goes by the name of religion is to a great extent unbridled human self-assertion in religious disguise." This is the sick religion that makes many people disbelievers in any religion.

But there is a healthy religion that produces meaningful service and redeems the hardest duty from its burdensomeness. From it comes a *strong giving-love* that is "a great and thorough good," as *The Imitation of Christ* so beautifully describes it:

By itself it makes everything that is heavy, light; and it bears evenly all that is uneven. For it carries a burden which is no burden, and

---

[11] Joshua Loth Liebman, *Peace of Mind* (New York: Simon and Schuster, 1946), p. 39.

[12] P. 271.

makes everything that is bitter, sweet and tasteful. . . . Love feels no burden, thinks nothing a trouble. Complains not of impossibility, for it thinks all things possible. . . . Though weary, it is not tired; though pressed, it is not straightened. [13]

Love Makes Duty Delightful

Seeing Myself

Service that is divinely beautiful and worth while is the *result* of getting your unlovely and unloved self off your hands. It cannot be beautiful and worth while when used as a means of escaping yourself. When duty is divine it is always a *product* or *result* of life freed of the inordinate demands of a twisted self-love. "Jesus, knowing . . . that he was come from God, and went to God; . . . took a towel." (John 13:3-4 K.J.V.) This is the order. *Not* "Jesus took a towel and proved that he was like God." He did not spend his last hours in trying to prove his worth to his disciples or to himself, but he gave himself to them with his thoughts concentrated on their needs. "If I then, your Lord and Teacher, have washed your feet, you also ought to wash one another's feet. . . . If you know these things, blessed are you if you do them."

Doing the Master's teaching is just another unlovely duty unless we share in the Master's secret. Beginning in his childhood days within the family in Nazareth, and wandering solitarily but not lonely on the hillsides and in the desert places nearby, Jesus grew up in the warm sense of belonging to the heavenly Father's love. At his baptism the inner voice assured him, "[You are] my beloved Son, with whom I am well pleased" (see Matt. 3:17). Jesus' loving service, even unto death, was not only possible but was redemptive in its effects because of his lifelong self-acceptance in his Father's love.

While we cannot duplicate the life of Jesus, we are privileged to follow him in "faith that works through love." Accepting the

[13]Thomas á Kempis, *The Imitation of Christ*, III. 5.

amazing love of God in forgiveness, we begin to understand and accept ourselves in spite of our unworthiness and failures. We begin to realize creative possibilities within us which are deeply real and possible as God sees them. Once we begin to believe in ourselves as God does, we will be able to believe in the possibilities wrapped up in the often unlovely lives of those about us and to care sincerely about helping them. As long as I am fighting a battle with myself and with others, trying to prove my superiority and lovableness, I am in no position to love anyone else. When I begin to say "no" to the false self-picture with its compulsive affections and twisted values, then I can say "yes" to the picture of myself which is in accord with reality. The values I seek in myself and others are always relative to the loving purposes of the Almighty Love.

Of course, if you believe in no law higher than your own and if the only values you accept are those considered good in any moment because *you* desire them, you will serve nothing that does not serve or exalt you. Then in your case, the criticism of the cynic, that all service is selfishly motivated, is certainly valid.

How sad, if we who accept the Christian teaching of the worth of each individual, spend our lifetimes constantly trying to prove to ourselves and others that we are worthy.

Service always degenerates into cynicism when the checks written on our bank account of love are marked "insufficient funds." On the other hand, when our bank account of love is unlimited, because we are drawing on the inexhaustible wealth of the love of Christ, we will find our duty no burden and our service a freedom!

Seeing My Brother

Service *that is divine is a result of seeing not only ourselves but others as loved by God and lovable in spite of their failures and wrongs.* Some unknown poet puts it this way:

I met a slender little maid, a rosy burden bearing.
"Is it not heavy, dear?" I said, as past me she was hurrying.

She looked at me with grave, sweet eyes, this fragile little mother,
And answered, as in swift surprise, "Oh, no, sire; it's my brother!"

We larger children toil and fret to help the old world onward;
Our eyes with tears are often wet, so slowly he moves sunward.
Yet did we all the secret seek of this dear little mother,
Unwearyingly we'd bear the weak, because he is our brother!

The trouble is in *seeing* our brother, even though he may live
in the same house and may be of the same blood. No one ever
loves even his own blood brother, much less the unlovely stranger
or the hateful enemy, unless and until he *sees* him with new eyes
of understanding.

Roxanne, the lovely young heroine in Joy Packer's delightful
story *Valley of the Vines,* describes this priceless gift belonging to
the young journalist, Hal, whom she loved. She is answering his
father's question as to why Hal is so beloved by the selfish young
ballerina, Alexa:

There could be many reasons—even apart from his attraction. . . .
He is a fine writer. He has your own gift of looking below the sur-
face. But what makes him lovable is that he looks for the good things—
the kind things—and so often he finds them in unexpected places. . . .
He finds the orchid growing in the rubbish heap; he makes you believe
in it. It's there, it's real—not just a fool's illusion. That's his extra
quality—his way of thinking—and living—and loving.[14]

Truly this ability to put ourselves in the other person's place, to
"sit where he sits," to look through his eyes, to understand how he
feels, is the source of our ability to love him. Such ability makes us
truly lovable as well as loving. Thus we can find the orchid growing in the rubbish heap that humanity often is!

How does this understanding vision of the secret of the lives of
others come to us?

[14] New York: J. B. Lippincott Co., 1955.

John Oxenham, in his poem on brotherhood, answers thus: *"If you want to find your brother, find yourself!"*

Compassionate understanding and concern for my brother is possible only as I see him as having experiences in common with mine. "You know the heart of the stranger," cries the Old Testament prophet, "for you were strangers in the land of Egypt; therefore love the stranger!" When one acts in anger toward you, hurtfully, spitefully, you will be able to love him only if you see that his anger is the result of deep anxiety or fear for his own security, the same kind of anxiety and fear that you yourself at times have had. When you identify his anxiety with yours, you may be able to bear his anger and even to do something positive in return—what Jesus meant by "turning the other cheek" and going the second mile. Thus you can love your neighbor *as you love yourself!*

Here we are obviously not talking about loving the false, prideful self whose will is twisted and warped even when it seeks the good, but the God-given, God-willed self.[15] These words of Meister Eckhart describe our need so well:

If you love yourself [in the right way], you love everybody else as you do yourself. As long as you love another person less than you love yourself, you will not really succeed in loving yourself, but if you love all alike, including yourself, you will love them as one person and that person is both God and man. Thus he is a great and righteous person who, loving himself, loves all others equally.[16]

Harry and Bonaro Overstreet go a step further than John Oxenham's formula. "If you want to find your brother, find yourself," yes; but *"If you want to find yourself, find your brother."* Obviously the two go together; you do not love your brother with-

---

[15] See treatment of self-love in *Conquering the Seven Deadly Sins*, pp. 16-17, 31, 47, 57, 80, 81, 111-13.
[16] *Meister Eckhart*, tr. R. B. Blakney (New York: Harper & Bros., 1941), p. 204.

out loving yourself, and you do not truly love yourself in the highest and best sense without loving your brother. It is only in the union of "I-Thou" that either "I" or "Thou" is complete!

Seeing God

Even this, however, is a long way from the fullest answer to our question. Jesus would complete the formula by adding a third affirmation, saying in effect: *"If you want to find yourself and your brother, be found of God!"* Here the sublime difference between acquisitive, possessive, desiring love and unmotivated, spontaneous, giving-love is most clearly seen. "For if you love [only] those who love you, what reward have you? Do not even the tax collectors do the same? And if you salute only your brethren, what more are you doing than others? Do not even the Gentiles do the same? You, therefore, must be perfect [in love], as your heavenly Father is perfect!" (Matt. 5:46-48.)

How is God perfect in his love for us? In the sense that his love is not conditioned by our worth, our goodness, but is freely given because it is his nature to love and he chooses to give his loving mercies to each of us to the limit of our willingness to receive them! "For he makes his sun rise on the evil and on the good, and sends rain on the just and on the unjust." (Matt. 5:45.)

If I am able to love others *only* insofar as I am able to see good in them—that is, to feel that they are worthy of my love and presumably may do something for me in return—I have missed the deepest significance of love that sets free and redeems. This kind of mutual backslapping abides only so long as things are going both ways. It cannot endure contradiction, disappointment, and betrayal, and therefore is inadequate for human life.

This kind of acquisitive love was the best that the world of Greek thought had known at the time of Jesus. Even Plato and Aristotle describe the highest kind of love as man's seeking, aspiring, hungering for the beauty in others and in God. In the pathway of this desiring-love, they taught, men may find duty and service to

91

man and God as a ladder upward out of selfishness to life. One must take his attention off himself and put it on the good in the universe about him.

"Man loves and desires only that which he wants and has not got," says Plato; "for who in the world would desire what he already has?" Thus loving is something for man and not for God. For the gods have everything they desire and need; therefore, they could not feel love; they could only be objects of love.[17] Thus love was to the ancient world, and still is to many in the modern world, an ever ascending path toward higher levels of appreciation and a desire for the good in those about us and in whatever there is in the nature of things which we call "God." There is, however, in this viewpoint, no sense of being the recipients of a mighty love which could give a deep sense of security and significance to our human loving. Much good has come into human life because of man's quest for love, but without cosmic grounding in the love of the Eternal, such loving is forlorn and pitiable.

It is nice and sensible, when the sun shines, to be kind and considerate, co-operative and outgoing in your thoughtfulness of others; but when the storms come and your little boat is threatened, unless you know the security of Eternal love, there is little likelihood that you will be too concerned about others.

The psychiatrist who examined hundreds of the American youth imprisoned by the Communists in Korea and China during the Korean War pointed to this significant fact: most of the men who cracked up, and/or abandoned their usual concern for their fellows, were men whose religious faith and disciplines had been nil, or at best only superficial. The few men who continued able to think of others and to serve their fellows under the primitive conditions of the concentration camps were generally those who possessed a deep religious faith and who had practiced a healthy kind of prayer and worship. They had been found by the love of the

[17] Cf. Anders Nygren, *Agape and Eros*, tr. Philip S. Watson (Philadelphia: Westminster Press, 1953), pp. 177-78.

Eternal and were able to love others even at the cost of great self-sacrifice.[18]

How can I love those who are unlovable, who are ugly and hateful, who seek to crucify me and all that I consider good? How can I love when loving is costly and requires the sacrifice of my desires, perhaps even my own life? Before these two questions, the love of mutual self-interest stops short. It has no answer.

On the other hand, when I stand before the cross on which the Son of God suffered the worst that human evil can inflict, and witness his love in which, by faith, I recognize the agape love of God poured out on those who crucify him, I enter into an entirely new dimension of love. When I see him forgiving them, serving them, redeeming them, I am awed by a Divine Love which, when compared to an acquisitive love, is like the light of the sun compared to a small candle in a dark room! The agape of God is poured out upon all mankind, even the worst and the lost. "Christ Jesus came to save sinners!" When I believe this includes me, and when by faith I accept his love, then I am able to pass it on to my neighbor.

I love others *not* in order that I may enjoy God, or earn his approval, or prove my superiority. I love because I have been loved and because it is my amazing privilege to be like God in this one respect: I may share in the creative, redeeming love that may help to bring my neighbors into the same blessedness of fellowship with God. It is not *my* love I give, but the love I have received from God. In this way each one of us, said Martin Luther, is called to be a Christ to his neighbor. Our relation to God and our fellow man its "likened to a tube, which by faith is open upwards, and by love downwards. All that a Christian possesses, he has received from God, from the Divine love; and all that he possesses he passes on in love to his neighbour." Then my love gives itself without any element of condescension or hurtful pride, "not where it finds a

[18] See *U.S. News and World Report*, February 24, 1956, pp. 56-72.

good to enjoy, but where it may confer good upon the poor and needy." [19]

"Jesus, knowing that he was come from God, and went to God; . . . took a towel . . ." This was the mighty secret of his love. He found himself and his brother in the love of the Eternal Father. His revelation of the agape love of God has put a new meaning and power into the old, old secret of "loving God with all your heart, soul, mind, and strength!" It is no longer a wistful quest looking upward at that which is infinitely desirable and lovable. It is now a thankful response of a grateful heart to the love of God that is poured out upon us through the Holy Spirit. What a difference in the two kinds of love!

True, in all high religions there have been flashes of understanding of this self-giving love of the Almighty. Rabindranath Tagore, the Indian poet, describes it thus:

Here is thy footstool and there rest thy feet where live the poorest, and lowliest, and lost.

The ability to love others as God loves us has been supremely the gift of those who have understood and accepted the revelation of the love of God in Christ. Tagore describes the difficulty of identifying himself with the love of God, whom he believes dwells with "the poorest, the lowliest, and the lost."

When I try to bow to thee, my obeisance cannot reach down to the depth where thy feet rest among the poorest, and lowliest, and lost

. . . .

My heart can never find its way to where thou keepest company with the companionless among the poorest, the lowliest, and the lost.[20]

What Tagore could not do, Jesus Christ could and did! In fellow-

[19] Nygren, op. cit., pp. 734-36.
[20] From "Here Is Thy Footstool," in Gitanjali. Copyright 1952 by The Macmillan Co. and used by their permission.

ship with him, countless thousands have found themselves identified with the Eternal Love and thus able to love themselves and others.

Why is it so many who profess to believe in the Christlike God and to love him have failed to make the kind of identification with their fellow men that Jesus made? Why is it that some few souls like Gandhi, who profess no understanding or acceptance of the theology of God revealed in Christ, nevertheless, have been able to be present with their fellows in genuine giving-love?

The most likely answer is to recognize that men like Gandhi have met the God of Christ in their experience, even though they have been unable to use the theological words that describe him. It is significant that the life and teachings of Jesus admittedly had a profound influence on Gandhi. Whether it be East or West, if the Aristotelian principle of finding God in right thought, through abstract reason, is followed, we may have orthodoxy of words and a heresy of spirit. The author of First John puts the real test of faith in Christ thus:

By this we may be sure that we know him, if we keep his commandments. He who says "I know him" but disobeys his commandments is a liar, and the truth is not in him; but whoever keeps his word, in him truly love for God is perfected. By this we may be sure that we are in him: he who says he abides in him ought to walk in the same way in which he walked. . . . For this is the message which you have heard from the beginning, that we should love one another. (2:3-6; 3:11.)

This has been the real genius of Christianity whenever it has been vital, from the early days of the first century through St. Francis, John Wesley, and Dwight L. Moody. "God is love, and he who abides in love abides in God, and God abides in him." (I John 4:16.)

The great Christlike lovers of God and man would heartily agree that "the love of God is neither the knowledge of God in thought, nor the thought of one's love of God, but the act of experiencing the oneness with God." [21] It is this paradoxical experience of millions of Christians which has provided them with the motive power for great loving: that which cannot be known (by thought, or logical processes of mind) is known in the experience of loving God and being loved by him. Theology, for such a person, becomes the best description possible to express in symbolic words what is inexpressible and unexplainable! As Harry Webb Farrington sings in the old Christmas hymn:

> I know not how that Bethlehem's Babe
>   Could in the God-head be;
> I only know the Manger Child
>   Has brought God's life to me.

> I know not how that Calvary's cross
>   A world from sin could free:
> I only know its matchless love
>   Has brought God's love to me! [22]

Who is God? The little child's question is still our deepest question.

God is the Nameless One! Upon this agree the best in our Hebrew-Christian tradition as well as the best in the Eastern religions. No word or name for God can ever give more than a clue to his infinite reality and nature. The dramatic story of Moses at the burning bush indicates this truth. God was revealed to Moses in his concern for his people in Egypt. But Moses said to God:

If I come to the people of Israel and say to them, "The God of your fathers has sent me to you," and they ask me, 'What is his name?' what shall I say to them?" God said to Moses, "I AM WHO I AM." ["I

[21] Fromm, op. cit., p. 78.
[22] Copyright by Harry Webb Farrington. Used by permission of the Hymn Society of America.

WILL BE WHAT I WILL BE."] And he said, "Say this to the people of Israel, 'I AM has sent me to you.'" (Exod. 3:13-14.)

God's name is: "I do not have a name"—for who can describe God? In essence this was Moses' insight.

Lao-tse, the great Chinese philosopher, put the same truth when he said, "The Tâo that can be [described] is not the enduring and unchanging Tâo. The name that can be named is not the enduring and unchanging name."

While we cannot describe him or name him in his fullness, we can experience him! This is the sublime truth of all effective religion. As Christians we believe that the best name that can be given to him is "Love" and that this love is revealed most fully in the unconditioned giving-love of Jesus Christ. Our acquaintance with his spirit through the records in the Gospels, through his records in the lives of his followers in every age, and through our own experience has brought us into the presence of the Mighty and Eternal Love! We know that these words are not enough for the Name of God; but we believe that who he is can be known in the communion of our spirits with his spirit and in our daily experiences as we follow him.

Perhaps the fullest embodiment of Christlike giving-love in our time is found in Albert Schweitzer, the Christian physician of the Lambaréné. The dedication of his unusual gifts and talents in the service of the neglected black men of Africa has been another fresh revelation of the meaning and value of human life. Why did he do it? Over and over he has brought his witness: because he believes that nothing but love is equal to the tragic needs of humanity today: "l'amour!" This is the dynamic ethic of Christianity:

According to the teaching of Jesus men are to be gripped by God's will of love, and must help to carry out that will in this world, in small things as in great things, in saving as in pardoning. To be glad instruments of God's love in this imperfect world is the service to which

97

men are called, and it forms a preparatory stage to the bliss that awaits them in the perfected world, the Kingdom of God.[23]

Schweitzer's own confession of faith is described in the well-known words:

He comes to us as One unknown, without a name, as of old, by the lake-side. He came to those men who knew Him not. He speaks to us the same word: "Follow thou me!" and sets us to the tasks which He has to fulfil for our time. He commands. And to those who obey Him, whether they be wise or simple, He will reveal Himself in the toils, the conflicts, the sufferings which they shall pass through in His fellowship, and, as an ineffable mystery, they shall learn in their own experience Who He is.[24]

So together with this great doctor, many other Christians of every age would say: We believe the Spirit that is in Christ is the revelation in human experience of the very nature of God, a revelation not in word but in life! As Paul says it so beautifully: "He is the image of the invisible God, the first-born of all creation. . . . For in him all the fullness of God was pleased to dwell!" (Col. 1:15-19.) Or in the words attributed to Jesus: "He who abides in me, and I in him, he it is that bears much fruit" (John 15:5). And "The fruit of the Spirit is love." (Gal. 5:22.)

Yes, God is infinitely beyond our highest thought. At best our words are but symbols of the ineffable glory and love that is God; but in our experience of love we find and know him! "No man has ever seen God; if we love one another, God abides in us and his love is perfected in us." (I John 4:12.) Let us therefore seek first and most ardently to meet him in our daily, hourly experience of communion and in the loving service to which he leads us, for "closer is He than breathing, and nearer than hands and feet."

[23] *Christianity and the Religions of the World*, tr. Johanna Powers (New York: Geo. H. Doran, 1923), p. 30.
[24] *The Quest of the Historical Jesus*, tr. W. Montgomery (New York: The MacMillan Co., 1906), p. 401.

Results of Experienced Love

The result of such union with the Christlike God is portrayed in countless lives, small and great. William Allen White, in an editorial of August, 1901, speaks of the longest funeral procession seen in Emporia, Kansas, in ten years. The procession followed the Rev. John Jones three long miles in the hot July sun out to Dry Creek Cemetery.

Now a funeral procession may mean little or much. When a rich and powerful man dies, the people play politics and attend his funeral for various reasons. But here was the body of a meek, gentle little old man —a man "without purse or script." He was a preacher of the gospel— but preachers have been buried before this in Emporia without much show of sorrow.

The reason so many people lined up behind the hearse that held this kind old man's mortality was simple: they loved him. He devoted his life to helping people. In a very simple way, without money or worldly power, he gave of the gentleness of his heart to all around him. We are apt to say that money talks, but it speaks a poverty-stricken language.

Hearts talk better, clearer, and with a wider intelligence. This old man with the soft voice and the kindly manners knew the language of the heart and he spoke it where it would give zest to joy. He worked manfully and with a will in his section of the vineyard, and against odds and discouragements he won time and again. He was infinitely patient and brave. He held a simple, old-fashioned faith in God and his loving kindness.

There is the secret! His simple faith in God was not theological abstraction but a conviction that opened his soul from its very center to the love of God. He was like Paul, "overmastered" by the love of Christ. "For the love of Christ controls us!" (II Cor. 5:14.)

For William Wilberforce also it was the experience of the love of God that produced the resolve "to live to the glory of God and

99

the good of my fellow creatures." The experience came to him while creeping by carriage over muddy, rutty roads, reading the New Testament in Greek and conversing about religion with his friend, the Rev. Mr. Isaac Milner, a "muscular, jovial Tarzan of a clergyman." It was this experience which took this brilliant young lawyer of twenty-five and made him, in spite of his stunted, feeble body racked by pain and illness, the one man most responsible for the abolition of slavery in the British Empire—a feat whose value can be seen only in comparison with the thousands of lives lost in the American Civil War to accomplish the same purpose. For forty-three years his concern for these black children of God led him on in parliament and in press and through endless speeches to stir up the consciences of his people. Twenty years after he undertook his crusade, the bill to abolish slavery in the British Empire finally passed, and he was given one of the greatest ovations ever seen in the House of Commons. But the battle was not won. Negroes were still being kidnaped, and in greater numbers than ever.

"I am sick of battle and long for quiet," Wilberforce said, "but I'll not leave my poor slaves in the lurch."

For twenty-six years he continued his struggle through physical pain and weariness and the loss of his home and financial support. But his was a joyous, vibrant love that made his service beautiful. At the end of his life he wrote, "Perhaps one reason my life has been spared so long is to show that a man can be as happy without a fortune as with one." [25]

The history of Christian influence is replete with its Albert Schweitzers, its John Joneses, and its William Wilberforces, who were "captured" by the love of Christ and whose lives of service were aflame with infinite beauty and joy. You cannot explain the dynamic love of such men apart from their experience of God. It

[25] *The Reader's Digest,* November, 1953, pp. 101-4.

surely must be said of these men and women as was said of their Lord: "Knowing that they had come from God and were going to God, they took a towel . . ."

Matthew Arnold, in his "East London," describes the humble city preacher whose services, though difficult and costly, were infinitely blessed and rewarding to himself as well as others:

> I met a preacher there I knew, and said:
> "Ill and o'er-worked, how fare you in this scene?"
> "Bravely!" said he, "for I of late have been
> Much cheered with thoughts of Christ, *the living bread."*

No duty will be delightful and no service rewarding that is not cheered by the presence and strength of "Christ the Living Bread," and by the sense that what I do is done in partnership with the Eternal and sustained by him.

Practical Applications

There are several practical applications of this sublime truth.

Recognize that you are hungry to "belong" to your family, your group, to the human race—this is what you were created for. Surely you want to be loved and appreciated, and this longing is right and proper. There is nothing wrong with the longing itself —only when it is exaggerated into a compulsion does it become deadly.

Discover in your past experiences the reasons why you have such an overpowering compulsion to find the approval of others so that even in your services you are like a little dog wagging its tail waiting for someone to pat you on the back—the reasons for "the delusions of duty" that keep you exhausted and miserable while you "carry the burdens" of those who don't really appreciate you or what you are doing for them. These reasons may be forgotten, but sometimes the help of a counselor, minister, doctor, or friend may help you to understand the experiences of rejection and isolation in your childhood that left you doubting your own worth.

Determine to accept no duty, to attempt no service, that is prompted by this abnormal compulsion that would attempt to force others to appreciate or recognize you. The difference in service motivated by the love of God and service motivated chiefly by such self-centered reasons is well illustrated in William Wilberforce. In the first period of his political life, before his experience of commitment to Christ, according to his own confession, "I did nothing [except that in which] my own distinction was my darling object." This kind of motive could never have freed the slaves, for it would never have set him free to love.

Choose those duties that are rightfully yours as a responsible person—a member of a home, a church, a community, a nation, a world—knowing that you cannot do everything, but choosing to do the thing for which you are best fitted and which, in the long run, can be of greatest service to your family and the world outside your family.

Take time out for meditation, worship, and prayer by which you "find yourself" and your brother in the true perspective and by which you are restored to a blessed sense of acceptance and relatedness to the love of God. For "goodness becomes gruesome unless wisdom guides"; and where duty is worshiped instead of God, there is "a psychic stench," a disgusting "odor of sanctity" [26] and self-pity that destroys the value of duty.

With the love of God capturing your spirit, you may be

> Maid of all work whether coarse or fine,
> A servant who makes service seem divine! [27]

When you find yourself exhausted and fed up with your service, let this be the warning signal to stop and think deeply about the

[26] Seabury, *op. cit.*, pp. 141-47.
[27] Henry Wadsworth Longfellow.

motive that led you on. Is it "the coercion of the world," the demands of "what-will-people-think," the compulsive and insatiable hunger to be approved and recognized? Anytime you are over-exhausted, with the exception of emergencies, you may know you are not doing your real duty out of love, but a false duty that will hurt and destroy your own self and probably not do much good to others.

Seek continually to find your true nature and the ways in which your particular talents can best serve the needs of others. "As it is not the duty of a cat to pull a plow or a horse to catch mice, you also have your field of effort, and no duty is yours that you are not built to undertake." [28] *When you are not fitted to do a service, it is never rightfully yours to do it!*

Remember that you are not God and therefore cannot do all the things you think you ought to do. You simply cannot fill all the obligations you feel called to fill. The servant of God who arrogantly tries to take the place of God is pitiably sick indeed, as in the story of Dick Sheppard, minister of St. Martin's-in-the-Fields in London, of whom I spoke in the preceding chapter. He had such a heavy schedule and so many obligations that they were weighing him down to the point where he was about to fall ill. One night he went to sleep and dreamed that he saw God receiving a telegram from earth, which said, "Dick Sheppard is about to be ill." He thought he saw God crush the telegram in his hands and walk up and down the parapets of heaven and say over and over again, "Dick Sheppard is about to be ill! What on earth am I going to do!" The scene was so funny Sheppard woke up laughing and was cured of his "delusion of duty" from that time on.

"God never asks so busy service that leaves no time for resting at his feet." No duty, no service is holy or blessed that keeps you so exhausted you have no time for keeping centered in the strong,

[28] Seabury, *op. cit.*, p. 151.

quiet love of the Eternal. "Blessed are they who are glad to have time to spend with God!" and join their little efforts to the mighty ongoing labors of the Eternal, whose magnificent purposes for mankind are forever sure and worthy of the services and love of our human lives. For "in his service is perfect freedom."

VI. Learning to Combat Evil with Love

Only a wise, strong love can face evil without fear or fawning and do the right and most helpful thing at the right time in the right spirit for all concerned. Only real love can save me from a spineless tolerance and an equally cruel intolerance.

There is a blessed intolerance, just as there is an equally blessed tolerance, made possible by the generous but unflinching demands of Christlike giving-love. It is love meeting evil without blinking, or bowing and scraping, or running, or giving up, or becoming a doormat for others' feet, or doing any other merely passive thing which is so often identified with Jesus' injunction to "love your enemies" (Matt. 5:44).

Here is the one most frequent misunderstanding of the place and attitude of Christlike love. That Jesus did not mean by these words that one merely "gives up" in the face of evil deeds is obvious from his own life. When he upset the tables of the money-changers in the temple and drove out those who made of God's house of prayer "a den of thieves," he was certainly not giving up to evil. And when he died on a cross between two thieves, the innocent suffering with the guilty, he was not supinely yielding himself in meek subjection to evil. In his encounters with evil, something of infinite good always came; and if we learn to love others as Christ also loves us, our encounters with evil will be positive—we will do the most creative thing that can be done under the circumstances. The apostle Paul's words to the Romans summarizes this possibility.

Let love be genuine; hate what is evil, hold fast to what is good. . . .
Bless those who persecute you; bless and do not curse them. . . .

Repay no one evil for evil, but take thought for what is noble in the sight of all. If possible, so far as it depends upon you, live peaceably with all. . . . Do not be overcome by evil, but overcome evil with good. (12:9-21.)

This is the very opposite of passively, supinely giving over to evil. Indeed we are to hate the evil and do all we can to destroy it.

It is of this blessed intolerance I sing, and not the kind of vicious intolerance described by Jonathan Swift's satiric words:

> We are God's chosen few
> All others will be damned;
> There is no place in heaven for you
> We can't have heaven crammed!

Nor am I speaking of the brand of intolerance portrayed by Dostoyevsky when he speaks of the baleful prostitution of mankind's desire for oneness which has led a good proportion of mankind to accept totalitarianism in government, society, business, and religion:

> For these pitiful creatures are concerned to find something that all would believe in and worship; what is essential is that *all* may be together in it. This craving for community of worship is the chief misery of every man individually and of all humanity from the beginning of time! For the sake of common worship they've slain each other with the sword. They have set up gods and challenged one another. "Put away your gods and come and worship ours; or we will kill you and your gods!" [1]

How tragic that the sense of oneness which we seek in the love for which we were created has been so twisted and mistaken! What a travesty—this requirement that everyone included in our love *must* have one point of view, "a general acquiescence to the mean"! Cer-

[1] Fyodor Dostoyevsky, *The Brothers Karamazov*, tr. Constance Garnett (New York: Random House, 1937), p. 262.

tainly Jesus would never call this kind of intolerance blessed, nor would any other understanding person. Obviously there is a tolerance which is a great virtue.

Tolerance May Be an Expression of Love

Jesus did not use any word similar to our word "tolerance." Perhaps there was no similar word in the Greek or the Aramaic of his time, though the attitude and spirit which we indicate thereby was most surely his. Luke relates the time when John came to Jesus with the complaint about a contemporary religious leader, "Master, we saw a man casting out demons in your name, and we forbade him, because he does not follow with us." Jesus was indignant and rebuked John and the other disciples for whom he was spokesman. "Do not forbid him; for he that is not against you is for you." (Luke 9:49-50.) He was saying, in effect, that there are many approaches to God, to truth and right; that just because a person doesn't make the same approach you do is no indication that he is against truth or God or right. Certainly you must not stop or hinder anyone who is earnestly seeking for light or endeavoring to minister sincerely to the needs of his fellows, even though he may be doing it in a different way from yours. What terrible evils would have been avoided in these two thousand years of Christian history if Jesus' words and spirit had been accepted, understood, and obeyed!

> Across the way my neighbor's windows shine,
> His roof-tree shields him from the storms that frown;
> He toiled and saved to build it, staunch and brown.
> And though my neighbor's house is not like mine,
> I would not pull it down!
>
> With patient care my neighbor, too, had built
> A house of faith, wherein his soul might stay,
> A haven from the winds that sweep life's way.

> It differed from my own—I felt no guilt—
> I burned it yesterday! [2]

Strong, wise love will surely seek to preserve, not destroy, the house of faith so precious to others.

It is well to note that one of the great Protestant principles is the right of private judgment, a re-emphasis on this spirit and teaching of Jesus. Martin Luther was calling for this precious right when he stood before the Diet of Worms to cry: "Unless I be convinced by Scripture or by reason, I can and will retract nothing; for to act against my conscience is neither safe nor honest. Here I stand!" But as one historian has pointed out, neither he nor the other reformers fully understood this principle:

> They knew what their own necessities demanded—but that was all. They raised the ensign of a free Bible in the face of Rome, but they speedily refused to allow others to fight under this banner as well as themselves. What Luther claimed for himself against Catholic authority, he refused to Carlstadt and to Zwingli. [3]

John Wesley was one of the first to see that if two men break fellowship because of a difference in opinions, then neither of them really believes in this right of private judgment, or tolerance. Mr. Wesley was proud of the fact that his Methodist societies were almost the only ones of his time which

> do not insist on your holding this or that opinion; but they think and let think. Neither do they impose any particular mode of worship; but you may continue to worship in your former manner, be it what it may. Now, I do not know any other religious society [or church] . . . wherein such liberty of conscience is now allowed, or has been allowed, since the age of the apostles. Here is our glorying; and a glorying peculiar to us! [4]

[2] Molly Anderson Haley, "Intolerance." Used by permission.
[3] Tulloch, *op. cit.*, pp. 168-73.
[4] *Journal of the Rev. John Wesley*, ed. Nehemiah Curnock (London: Epworth Press, 1938), VII, 389.

As the Methodist societies grew strong and the fellowship enthusiastic and warm, Mr. Wesley was deeply concerned that his people should not become narrowly intolerant of others. In a letter to Vincent Perronet in 1748, he wrote: "The thing which I was greatly afraid of all this time, and which I resolved to use every possible method of preventing, was a narrowness of spirit, a party zeal . . . that miserable bigotry which makes many so unready to believe that there is any work of God but among themselves." To cure this he recommended the regular reading of the "work which God is carrying on in the earth . . . , not among us alone, but among those of various opinions and denominations." [5]

Tolerance has been one of the great American virtues. The emphasis could be said to have begun with Roger Williams, who, denied religious liberty in Salem, made that long trek through the bitter winter to Providence, Rhode Island. Here, at the cost of great suffering, he established the first place in America, and in all the world of his day, where religious freedom and liberty of conscience were exalted. The framers of our Constitution wrote into our national philosophy the right of freedom of thought, speech, and worship; the freedom to think and let think; to speak what we wish to speak. In America tolerance has been lifted to the position of a noble virtue. Of this you and I can be rightly proud.

The best definition I know of Christian tolerance is that of Phillips Brooks:

Tolerance expressed a perfectly legitimate and honorable relation between opposite minds. I disagree with my friend. But I respect him; I want him to be true to his convictions, yet I claim the right and duty of trying to persuade him to my belief. Tolerance is the meeting in perfect harmony of earnest conviction and personal indulgence! [6]

This we would not want to lose. Nothing would be more catas-

[5] Henry Carter, *The Methodist Heritage* (Nashville: Abingdon Press, 1951), p. 206.
[6] *Selected Sermons*, ed. William Scarlett (New York: E. P. Dutton & Co., 1949).

trophic than a renewal of bigotry, pride, and selfishness. We need to preserve in our civilization the right of private judgment. We must all fight and live for this right of others to differ with us and for our right to differ with them.

Broad-mindedness Without Love Destroys

The sad fact is that the true meaning of the word "tolerance" is being perverted and prostituted by a great many Americans today. Our national character, at least a great part of it, is beginning to resemble the character in John Bunyan's *Pilgrim's Progress*: "Mr. Facing-Both-Ways." Too many of us are trying to ride the fence. Evil is so popular, dressed up in such respectable clothes, we are loath to oppose it. After all we are doing the customary thing so as not to be different, so as to be like other people! We are on the fence so often we get ourselves into one mess after another. "In the name of an easy tolerance and under the popular banner of broad-mindedness . . . we have all but arrived at the place where we imagine that virtue consists in having the kind of mind that never shuts a door upon anything, the kind of spirit that is shocked by nothing," writes Robert Goodrich. He quotes from *Woman's Home Companion* an arresting article, by Mrs. Elizabeth Massey Hill, entitled "Don't Call Me Broad-minded":

To be broad-minded seems to be the most desirable trait possible today. Beat your wife if you like; steal if you must; but never deviate from the path of broad-mindedness. It amounts to a fetish and I for one am sick of it.

I cannot discover a single thing—except Communism, of course—which we are not supposed to tolerate. Did your neighbor cheat his brother's widow out of her inheritance? Poor thing, he must have been the victim of some childhood insecurity which left him with a pathological craving for money.

Has your best friend run off with your husband? You must realize that monogamy is an unnatural state for the male animal and most likely your friend's mother didn't teach her when she was small that it is rude to grab. You must get a divorce on polite grounds, give a party

110

for the happy pair . . . and teach Junior to call the lady "aunt." . . .

Well, I am now through being tolerant. It seems to me that a bit of insistence on the old-fashioned virtues might be a healthy change. . . . Even in smaller matters I am quitting the broad-minded group. . . . There is a line, and I am going to draw it.

So from now on, call me anything else you like, but don't call me broad-minded! Those are fighting words! [7]

We certainly need to take a fresh look at our cult of broad-mindedness and tolerance. We need to see that there are two kinds of tolerance: the blessed and the deadly, the Christlike and the vicious.

Now Jesus was warning us against the deadly kind of broad-mindedness and the disaster of following it when he said, "Enter by the narrow gate; for the gate is wide and the way is easy, that leads to destruction, and those who enter by it are many. For the gate is narrow and the way is hard, that leads to life, and those who find it are few." (Matt. 7:13.)

Like the prophets before him, Jesus was extremely "narrowminded"—if you want to call it that—when it came to justice, mercy, truth, and love. His was a strong love, a powerful kindness. He was terrible in his tenderness. We have had pictured too often by some modern writers a Jesus who was a "genial good fellow," who forgave everybody from the woman taken in adultery, the lying Simon Peter, the stealing tax collector Zacchaeus, to the thief on the cross. But what we have forgotten is that this forgiveness has upon it the costliness of the cross; the indignation of the one who could drive out from the temple the money-changers who made excessive profits, a "racket" out of poor people's desire for worship; and the intolerance of one who could not stomach the hypocrisy and double-dealing of the Pharisees, who "cleanse the outside of the cup and of the plate, but inside they are full of extortion and rapacity" (Matt. 23:25).

[7] Used by permission of the author and *Woman's Home Companion*.

As the result of his intolerance of evil, they killed him! We must never forget that. But we must also remember that though his method of meeting evil did not save him from the cross, it did have its saving influence from which mankind can never escape. Here on the cross is the drama of redemptive love that can be re-enacted in every moment when the soul of man is confronted by threatening and treacherous evil. Not the soft, easy answer, but the hardheaded, truth-regarding, creative way of combating evil!

This is all rather confusing, some of you are thinking. At one time Jesus says, "He that is not against you is for you" (Luke 9:50); and another time he says, "He who is not with me is against me" (Luke 11:23). What does he mean?

Real Love Makes Intolerance a Virtue

When is it good to be broad-minded and when should we be narrow-minded? Generous but strong love has the only effective answer.

It is good to be broad-minded when our tolerance permits others to differ from us in opinions, customs, and habits. Only then can there be diversity and progress in our human relationships. What a pitifully ugly and boring world, where everyone lived alike, thought alike, and worshiped alike! We may disagree with others and try to persuade them of the wrongness of their ideas and ways, but when we love them we set them free, even in their wrongness —that is, unless we are sure their freedom is a menace to the whole community. It is in this climate of tolerant freedom that personality grows best. Such is our Hebrew-Christian heritage.

On the other hand, tolerance is an evil when we are so broad-minded that it makes no difference what anyone believes or does so long as he doesn't get in our way. Such indifference reduces truth, right, justice, and mercy to a pale nonentity, a matter of little or no import, and is the wide, easy way to destruction.

The worst threat to our human welfare today is not Communism or Fascism, as dangerous as they are, but rather the indifferent tolerance that believes nothing with conviction and takes no stand on any issue, for to do so will "hurt business," "is unsafe," and the like! This is the great danger of the free world, as Sara Henderson Hay pictures it in her poem "Heresy Indeed":

> It is a piteous thing to be
> Enlisted in no cause at all,
> Unsworn to any heraldry;
> To fly no banner from the wall,
> Own nothing you would sweat or try for,
> Or bruise your hands or bleed or die for.
>
> .   .   .   .
>
> To take the smooth and middle path,
> The half-heart interest, the creed
> Without extreme of hope or wrath,
> Ah, this were heresy indeed
> That all God's pity will not stay for,
> And your immortal soul will pay for.[8]

If I had to choose between the easy tolerance of an Erasmus who was "without any very living and powerful faith, cool, cautious, subtle and refined, more anxious to expose a sophism, or point a barb at some folks than to fight manfully against error and sin," [9] and the earnestness and longing for certainty of Martin Luther, even with his exaggeration and intolerance, certainly I would choose the intolerance of Luther. Neither spirit, however, describes the attitude of strong, wise love, which insists on finding the truth, but realizes that no expression of the truth can ever be but a feeble symbol of the Highest Reality.

There is, nevertheless, a need for the right kind of intolerance, for there is a narrowness about truth that calls for reverence and respect. The truths about electricity and atomic fission are exceeding-

[8] Reprinted from *This, My Letter* by Sara Henderson Hay, by permission of the author.

[9] Tulloch, *op. cit.*, p. 106.

ly narrow. Vary only a millionth of an inch, disregard the truth in the smallest way, and suffering and destruction follow. So it is with the truth about life.

This is what Jesus meant by "Enter by the narrow gate. . . . For the gate is narrow and the way is hard, that leads to life, and those who find it are few." Look at two of these truths that are exceedingly narrow: (1) "Whoever would save his life will lose it; and whoever loses his life for my sake, he will save it." (Luke 9:24.) That is to say, self-centered living is going to destroy you and your happiness and your home. Unless you put God into the center of your life, eventually you will find utter futility and destruction. (2) "Love God and your neighbor supremely." Human life is frustrating, defeating, evil, when lived contrary to this truth of loving relationship with God and our brothers.

There is truth about which you cannot afford to be tolerant and broad-minded. If you know your house is on fire, you "do not sit by tolerantly and give a moderate alarm," says William Lloyd Garrison in the introductory editorial in the first issue of the *Liberator*. He was crying out against the evils of slavery.

Some will criticize me for my severity of language. . . . I will be as harsh as truth and as uncompromising as justice. On this subject I do not wish to think, or speak, or write with moderation. No! No! . . . Tell a man to moderately rescue his wife from the hands of the ravisher; tell the mother to gradually extricate her babe from the fire into which it has fallen; but urge me not to use moderation in a cause like the present. I am in earnest—I will not excuse—I will not retreat a single inch—AND I WILL BE HEARD! [10]

We need more of this kind of loving intolerance today: a powerful, growing, persistent intolerance of the false, unloving, and unjust. We need men and women who will not be moderate or tolerant of ideas and acts that limit or destroy the dignity and free-

[10] Quoted by Ralph Korngold, *Two Friends of Man* (Boston: Little, Brown & Co., 1950).

dom of human spirit. *Tolerance is dangerously vicious when it is an expression of careless unconcern for the truth upon which the well-being of ourselves or of others depends.*

This truth of strong love is aptly put by Father Mapple in his great sermon to the whalers in the little chapel by the sea in Herman Melville's *Moby Dick*:

Woe to him who seeks to pour oil upon the waters when God has brewed them into a gale! Woe to him who seeks to please rather than to appal! Woe to him whose good name is more to him than goodness! Woe to him who, in this world, courts not dishonour! Woe to him who would not be true, even though to be false were salvation!

Intolerance is an expression of wise love when it refuses to countenance or excuse the evils in our lives, our homes, and our society simply because they are the customary things. Just because a thing is a custom does not make it right. It is true that customs enable us to keep the good of the centuries, but on the other hand, they may also cause us to keep the evil and to be unwilling to see it or get rid of it.

Large numbers of babies in the African bush die each year because their parents blindly follow custom. For generations these people have spread dried cow dung on the floors of their huts. It has the advantage of keeping down the dust and is an established, time-honored custom; but the custom is wrong because it is contrary to the truth that such floor coverings breed bacteria often fatal to small children. The desire for conformity is a powerful instinct within all of us and is a good thing up to a certain point; but when the desire to be like others leads us to accept habits and customs that are hurtful and destructive, to continue tolerating them is deadly. *Blessed are the ones who are intolerant of the customary when experience and common sense show that the customary is hurtful and dangerous.*

Much of the good in our civilization was not brought about by conformists, but by the nonconformists who learned to question and defy evil customs and practices which are contrary to the truth of God.

Why do you go along with the customs in your life and home that you know are not conducive to the spiritual and physical well-being of yourself and your loved ones? Perhaps in the name of tolerance, broad-mindedness—"everybody's doing it." If so, these words of Ogden Nash are an appropriate rebuke:

> Sometimes with secret pride I sigh
> To think how tolerant am I;
> Then wonder which is really mine:
> Tolerance, or a rubber spine?[11]

Well, which is yours? Are you rubber-spined about a thing just because it is customary? When tolerance is just another name for a rubber spine, we are on the broad road that leads to destruction. *Whenever tolerance is an excuse for carelessness or practiced in the name of custom, it is an evil reflection of the absence of genuine love.* Readers of movie magazines may recall the story of the husband of a movie queen who, when told that his wife was divorcing him to marry a movie star, threw up his hands in indifference and laughed as he said, "Oh well, I hope they will be happy." He was not tolerant, he was simply unconcerned.

Are you so broad-minded that as a citizen you shrug your shoulders with a tolerant smile when there is evidence of corruption and graft in government leaders? If so, you are joining in pushing our country on the way to loss of democracy and the destruction of our rights.

Beatitudes for the Lovingly Intolerant

May I suggest an additional new set of beatitudes that describes the spirit of Christlike love in this respect:

[11]From *I'm a Stranger Here Myself* by Ogden Nash. Copyright 1936 by the Curtis Publishing Company. First appeared in *The Saturday Evening Post*. By permission of Little, Brown and Company.

Blessed are the parents who are intolerant of their children's failure to obey and respect the laws of the home when those laws are based on the good of all concerned.

I am thankful for what might well be called the blessed intolerance of my mother, who disciplined us when we failed in our family obligations or hurt each other in carelessness or anger. Any person who learns to respect and care for the rights of others has had to learn it from his parents or someone else who was lovingly intolerant of his transgressions.

"My mother found it necessary to cut deeply into my character with the scalpel of courage and righteous judgment," writes Bishop Austin Pardue. One evening, while he was in his teens, she had told him he must return home immediately after work. He agreed, but instead he hung around a Chicago street corner as on other days. When he arrived home, his mother greeted him with intolerant indignation, or "righteous anger," and told him to pack up his clothes and leave. "She told me that the time apparently had come when I was making the rules of conduct for our home, and therefore I had to live elsewhere. I was stunned." She explained that until he was of age, he would have to abide by the rules of the home or live elsewhere. Young Austin Pardue left the house and walked the streets for several hours until, filled with contrition, he returned home and promised thereafter to "obey the rules of the house which were fair and just." [12]

Blessed are the members of society who are intolerant of those who flagrantly disregard the laws of society upon which the well-being of all depends.

This sounds like a truism, but it is not—at least not in America today. In this age of humanitarianism, we have the era of "the juvenile criminal," says Judge Leibowitz, one of the outstanding juvenile judges in one of our great cities, "and I emphasize the word 'criminal.' . . . Mere youngsters are holdup men, armed with loaded guns,

[12] *A Right Judgment in All Things* (Greenwich, Conn.: Seabury Press, 1954), pp. 156-57.

iron knuckles, switchblade knives, daggers. . . . Crimes such as rapes, burglaries, felonious assault, arson, dope peddling [are committed by youngsters] from twelve years [of age] and upwards. The really alarming feature is that these dangerous youngsters [are] turned loose time after time with hardly a slap on the wrist." "As a result," says Ruth Alexander, in a speech before a group of educators in Chicago, "more than 71% of all arrests are repeats. . . . Of the more than half million youngsters (10-17) who were arrested in 1954, this group accounted for nearly 40% of the arrests for all serious crimes reported by 1,389 cities." She emphasized one of the factors in this appalling record: that too often,

even at the risk of discrediting the judiciary itself, everything is done to save the children from the consequences of their acts. I know of no other group that rates such privilege. . . . But the delinquent has no reason to be afraid. As one adorable baby-faced blond said, when asked if he thought he could get away with his fifth armed robbery, aged fourteen—"Why not? I always have!"

But that's the catch. There comes a time when the clock strikes twelve and he can no longer get away with it. It is not fair to the child to let him escape punishment up to a certain time of day, and then . . . give him the works for crime. He should have been punished at the start, *according to his act—not according to his birthday*.[13]

There are other and more basic causes of juvenile crime, as Ruth Alexander herself would point out, as well as many others who like her have been dealing with juvenile delinquency.[14] Most delinquent youth are lacking in meaningful relationships to serve as an adequate model for their striving. Without such relationships, they have a twisted self-image and as a result do foolish and often criminally hurtful things in order to gain from the gang the recogni-

[13] From *Vital Speeches of the Day*, XXII (May 15, 1956), 463-64. Used by permission of the author.

[14] See Richard V. McCann, *Delinquency: Sickness or Sin?* (New York: Harper & Bros., 1957).

tion and approval which they lack from wise, loving parents or friends. It is certain that tougher methods cannot reach this deeper cause of delinquency; nevertheless, we cannot be heedlessly tolerant just because these are children, or encourage the continuance of their crimes by soft treatment. True, the only way to change them is through love; but it is a strong rather than a weak and soft love that will do it. And it will require something more than adding to the police force. It will take the concerted effort of many Christlike persons in every community to find and befriend these youth and give them a new self-image to strive for. It will also take the costly methods of slum clearance and other means of helping the families of these children, wherever possible, to establish genuine homes.

Blessed are those who are intolerant of wrong and injustice anywhere in the world. This applies to our national and international relationships. There is a cynical diplomacy being used by governments today which disregards the evils of their allies so long as they co-operate in opposing a hostile nation. Such policy is not diplomacy but the worst kind of foolishness. It was our tolerance of the militarism of Japan, our willingness to trade scrap iron to be shot into other people, that helped make possible the use of this same scrap iron in the shells that killed thousands of our own boys.

Christopher Fry's words, in *A Sleep of Prisoners*, present the prophetic challenge of strong love for humanity in this our day of H bombs and selfish indifference:

> The human heart can go to the lengths of God.
>
> . . . .
>
> Thank God our time is now when wrong
> Comes up to face us everywhere,
> Never to leave us till we take
> The longest stride of soul men ever took.
> Affairs are now soul size.
>
> . . . .
>
> . . . . It takes

So many thousand years to wake,
But will you wake for pity's sake? [15]

Affairs are now soul size indeed! And we've got to go far enough
in our exploration into the love of God to be intolerant of those
things that hurt and maim our lives and our society, in our own
nation and in the nations of the world. But this intolerance is a
loving wisdom that takes the steps necessary for building right relationships where there has been only the wrong.

The healing powers of divine love can make a bridge between
warring families, races, and countries. This is our great hope, the
only way peace will ever come. If, when you are wounded by
others, even though crippled and hurt so badly you must crawl
to them, you go to them and bind up their wounds, they may do
the same for you. But whether they do or not, you have erased
the pain of selfish hate and isolation and have found the greatest
power on earth: the power of giving-love. Sometimes the love is
not returned—instead they put you on a cross as they did Jesus.
But his cross became the most powerful emblem ever known to
man. Greater than the power of all the Genghis Khans, the Caesars
and Napoleons, the Hitlers and the Stalins, whether in world or
private history, is the cross of Christ. No wonder Paul cried, "Far
be it from me to glory except in the cross of our Lord Jesus Christ,
by which the world has been crucified to me, and I to the world"
(Gal. 6:14).

Now when wrong comes up to face us everywhere, we must be
ready to take the longest stride of soul men ever took—the stride
of strong, wise love that finds the mean between the two extremes
of indifferent tolerance and blind, cruel intolerance, that goes
the second and third and tenth mile with a positive love able to
redeem the evildoer. Thus we overcome evil with good (Rom.
12:21) and fulfill Jesus' promise, "Blessed are you when men re-

[15] From *A Sleep of Prisoners.* Copyright 1951 by Christopher Fry. Reprinted by
permission of Oxford University Press, Inc.

vile you and persecute you. . . . Rejoice and be glad." Why should I be glad when I encounter evil? Because here is the opportunity to help another in one of life's profoundest ways; and because in so meeting evil with love, I may lose something of my false self in the process and become a more mature person.

Love Can Use Force for Good

Obviously, when we encounter evil, we do not always help save the evildoer. Oftentimes he is too far gone in sickness of mind and soul—in false pride, greed, lust, envy, or jealousy. Then if we truly love as a member of the family of God, we will seek, if possible, to restrain him from hurting others. Some from honest conviction believe that force can never be used by Christlike love. From my viewpoint this attitude comes dangerously near to becoming a rigid principle. An unqualified obedience to such a "good principle" may add to the suffering and hurt of others and therefore become another evil.

To deal adequately with the problem of the use of force in combating evil would require a whole book within itself. Hence it is only possible in the limits of this treatment to point in the direction of its solution. The use of force, whether in city, state, national, or international police action, can never be considered as an adequate answer to the evil. It is only a holding operation at best but it may be carried out in loving consideration of the welfare of the most people. Nevertheless, it still must wait for the more positive action of love to enter and redeem the situation. Surely, intolerance of war as an acceptable method of settling international disputes is as much a part of Christlike love as was intolerance of dueling or gang fights in the olden days. A war, little or big, never settles anything. Only strong, wise love can heal the wounds and bring justice in human relationships.

How do we express intelligently and helpfully our intolerance of the wrongs all about us? This is one of the most difficult of questions. In a sense, this is one of the major purposes of this entire book,

121

in each chapter of which the spirit and method of true goodness is described.

There are at least three principles of real love that help us define the most creative ways of meeting this problem of evil.

I. Intolerance with Tender Kindness

First, my intolerance, even when it is legitimately exercised against great wrongs, is never blessed if it is primarily a means of flaunting my ego, of proving my superiority, or demonstrating my power. Intolerance is not blessed even though its goal is good, except when practiced by strong love.[16] It goes without saying that Austin Pardue's mother would have driven her son away from home to stay if she had not shown then and on many other occasions that she was not thinking only of herself, but of his well-being. *It is "tender kindness" like unto God's that alone can keep a righteous intolerance from being a deadly evil.*

II. Intolerance with Genuine Humility

Second, intolerance is always an evil, even though applied to the removal of recognized evils, if it is not accompanied by true humility. It is by what Joshua Liebman calls resisting "the temptation to private imperialism" that we make good and helpful our justly intolerant opposition to the wrong and evil about us. "We best show our love for our neighbors when we achieve an inner tolerance for the uniqueness of others," and this must be done even while we are opposing the evils they represent. "The world is full of private imperialists, those who cannot conquer any foreign territory but who make those nearest and dearest to them pay tribute all of their lives to their tyrannical decrees." [17] Our intolerance of the wrongs about us must be redeemed by our love of the wrong-doer. Any use of the right to dominate and control others is a des-

---

[16] Several aspects of this have already been discussed in Chap. III, "Learning to Give Love."
[17] *Op. cit.*, p. 74.

perate evil. Only in the humility of love can we be truly helpful.

Beware lest you think that you are infinitely more righteous than others when you make such decisions. You must have the confidence that God has shown you the truth but that you yourself are still filled with human frailty and while asking for mercy on your own behalf, proceed with such light as you may have to follow through, awaiting whatever may come in the name of Christ.[18]

One of the best illustrations of this humility is in a recent Broadway play, *Inherit the Wind,* which dramatizes the famous Scopes trial in the little city of Dayton, Tennessee, in July, 1925. Here William Jennings Bryan and Clarence Darrow fought the battle over evolution in "The Monkey Trial," as it was called. Drummond, in the characterization of Clarence Darrow, shows up the inherent bigotry of Matthew Harrison Brady's character in the William Jennings Bryan role, breaking his spirit and winning the case before the jury of public opinion, even if not before the legal jury present. Brady and other literalists who were determined to punish the young physics teacher who dared to teach evolution in the schools were right in their intolerance toward a teaching they believed to be hurtful. They had a perfect right to speak their minds, but their intolerance was hurtful because it was touched with bigotry. In the long run their intolerance did their cause more harm than good. Drummond is not only clever, but possessed with a blessed intolerance. Though fighting the bigotry of his opponents, he continues to have a genuine respect and love for Brady, much to the disgust of the young Boston reporter, who includes the man in his hatred of his wrongs.

Drummond's opportunity comes to break the proud spirit of Brady when the latter declares that he knows God didn't speak to Charles Darwin "because God tells me to oppose the evil teachings of that man."

[18] Pardue, *op. cit.,* p. 58.

"Oh. God speaks to you," says Drummond.

"Yes."

"He tells you exactly what's right and what's wrong?"

"Yes."

"And you act accordingly?"

"Yes."

"So you, Matthew Harrison Brady, through oratory, legislation, or whatever, pass along God's orders to the rest of the world! [Here the audience begins to laugh.] Gentlemen, meet the 'Prophet from Nebraska'!" [Brady's oratory is unassailable, but his vanity—exposed by Drummond's prodding—is only funny. The laughter is painful to Brady.]

"Is that the way of things? God tells Brady what is good! To be against Brady is to be against God! [More laughter] . . . The Gospel according to Brady! God speaks to Brady, and Brady tells the world! Brady, Brady, Almighty!" [19] [It is here that Brady breaks up and has to be carried away.]

Such intolerance is always self-defeating. To set myself up as God, intentionally or not, to refuse others the right to believe God has spoken to them, is bigotry. It cannot last. To believe that God speaks only to Brady, and not to Darwin or Cates, is egotism of the highest order. Brady and every other mistaken person has the right to fight for what he believes is right, but only in true humility and openness can such intolerance be fruitful. Intolerance, even in the cause of right, is likely to be blessed only as it is practiced by one whose resources of humility, faith, and love come from God.

Contrast this egoistic intolerance with that of the great German Christian Otto Karl Kiep, who resisted the Nazi falsehood among his people. He was arrested and sentenced to die, but while awaiting execution he wrote a verse which is paraphrased thus:

This is the meaning of prayer: to summon one's best strength in humility; to gain a sense of perspective in which all things are rightly seen; to stop doing what one has foolishly begun; and to place one's trust in the guidance of Him who is on High. . . . Every individual or people will be judged according to this standard. My dear country, realize this truth, and there will come to you salvation and a time in which your suffering will be forgotten.[20]

This is truly blessed and Christlike intolerance—to summon one's best strength in humility, to see things in the right perspective, and to trust the guidance of God! As the old hymn by John S. B. Monsell calls us:

> Fight the good fight with all thy might!
> Christ is thy strength, and Christ thy right;
> Lay hold on life, and it shall be
> Thy joy and crown eternally.

III. Intolerance with Forgiveness

There is the one last principle that must be applied, or any effort to combat evil ends in hurt for all concerned. Even while the evil is being met and overcome with the wisest means at my disposal, I must have a positive outgoing, forgiving love for the evildoer. "Hate the sin but love and forgive the sinner"—so runs the old maxim. It sounds very orthodox and proper; but is isn't quite that simple. Indeed, it is extremely difficult for me to differentiate between the evil and the evil's agent, especially when I am in the throes of my own or others' suffering caused by the evildoer!

"Asking me to forgive my enemy is like asking me to take a trip to the moon! Theoretically it is feasible. Practically it is impossible!" Thus the average man will say. Certainly it is impossible on the normal level of self-centered existence (if you can call *that* normal). Even on the highest level of desiring-love it is most unlikely, as pointed out in Chap. V.

[20] *Dying We Live*, ed. H. Gollwitzer, *et al.*, tr. Reinhard C. Kuhn (New York: Pantheon Books, 1956), p. xxi.

Only in the relationship of real love, upward toward God and outward toward others, is it truly possible and likely. Agape love that loves as God loves is in an entirely different dimension from eros love that loves only that which is lovable and worthy. Stand in the light of forgiving love that comes down from the cross, that shines from the face of Stephen, Polycarp, and the other martyrs, that glows with a heavenly radiance from the lives of Joan of Arc, Edith Cavell, William Booth, Abraham Lincoln, and the hundreds of modern Stephens and Polycarps in Nazi and Communist concentration camps of our own times, and you will know forgiving love is powerfully real and vital. You will know that it is the truly normal way for children of the eternal Father to live and meet evil and death!

Dying We Live, an inspiring volume from which we have just quoted the testimony of Otto Karl Kiep, contains the last letters and testaments of a group of noble spirits executed in the various Nazi prisons during the war. In these letters is to be found over and over the testimony to this possibility of forgiving love as an actuality, performed without any sense of straining or hard duty, but as a lovely fruit of the Spirit within.

How does one love his hateful enemy with such a positive, creative, redeeming love? Here we must be as specific as possible, first in saying what is not involved in forgiving-love and then in saying what is.

Forgiving another in the love with which God has loved me does not require me to love the false self, the hardened shell of compulsive affections and twisted values out of which has issued the hurt to me or others. God does not love this mass of falsehood and stupidity. Hence, it will not be necessary or desirable for me to *like* what I see of my enemy. Love as an affection, desiring the beautiful in another, is certainly impossible toward my enemy whom I see at his worst.

On the other hand, love as a steady acceptance of the other person, regardless of his acts, as "God's other child" in a "far country," lost and away from his true homeland, is grandly possible. Evelyn Underhill defined charity—God's agape coming through me to others—as "universal and deliberate kindness." But it is more than a kindness toward those I know and like; it includes all those people I don't like and whom I may not know at all.

Loving the evildoers requires understanding them and their motivations as much as possible, recognizing their anxieties, pressures, and compulsions that are akin to mine and that drive them to evil. Mine may be of a different stamp, but both theirs and mine originate from the same prideful self-love. This will help, but within itself it is not enough to enable me to love them.

Again, genuine love is not purely a matter of feeling. It would require waiting until doomsday for most of us ever to whip up a feeling of affection for certain hard characters we know!

It is not required that I like, or approve, or hold an affectionate feeling, or even that I fully understand my enemy in order to forgive him. It does require one central thing: an act of the will, as I accept him as my brother in the family of God—a prodigal, rebellious, unloving brother, yes, but loved by God and therefore loved by me. *Forgiving love is an attitude and an act of good will* that leads me to do two very definite things:

1. *Seek to restrain him from injuring others and myself, if possible, without taking on myself the responsibility that belongs to God and/or the government.* Most of the time the restraining of the evildoer is not my responsibility. It belongs to the officers of the government, who under most circumstances are "God's servant for your good," as the apostle Paul describes them, who "[do] not bear the sword in vain; [they are] the servant[s] of God to execute his wrath on the wrongdoer" (Rom. 13:4). It is surely God's intention that the governing authorities should be the ones to restrain the wrongdoer. The "wrath of God," unlike the "wrath of men," as it is most often seen, is not egoistic. It is simply that unrelenting good will of God for his children's good which stands squarely in the way of self-willed men who seek their own ends regardless of

the good of their fellows. As described in the preceding paragraphs concerning the use of force, love which includes the good of all must include the restraining of evil.

This restraining of evil, however, can never be a personal issue with anyone who truly shares the love of God. "Vengeance is mine, I will repay, says the Lord." (Rom. 12:19.) Personal spite, malice, and the desire to get even are unworthy of one who himself has been forgiven. Over and over, the Gospels record Jesus insisting that the exacting, unforgiving soul is in an impossible situation. The parable of the unforgiving debtor (Matt. 18:23-35), who was forgiven a large sum but would not forgive his debtors their small sums, and was consigned to "the jailers, till he should pay all his debt," is symbolic of the folly of the hard, vengeful spirit. The madness of a Hamlet killing not only the guilty murderer but also the ones he is supposed to love most is an accurate description of the futility of revenge, even in the name of love!

2. *Forgiving-love as an attitude and an act of good will leads me not only to renounce vengeance or a vengeful spirit, but positively to say and do everything in my power to help my enemy "come to himself," to recognize his sin against love, and to accept his true relationship with God and with others.*

How do I come to possess this attitude of undiscourageable good will? Let me illustrate with the story of a Chinese Christian whom Bishop W. Y. Chen, of the Methodist Church in China, met on the streets in a Chinese city one day shortly after the bombings by the Japanese. The man was weeping and would not be consoled.

"I have lost my wife, my children, and my home—all wiped out by one bomb! I have nothing to live for. I cannot decide whether to take the way of the cross and commit suicide or go out and get vengeance on the enemy."

Bishop Chen hurried to explain to the distraught man that suicide was not the way of the cross. There is a third way: the way of love—accepting the love of God, which included the Japanese as well as himself, and seeking to do everything possible to translate that love into action in everyday life.

A few months later the bishop came across this same man but he now had an entirely different demeanor. Indeed, he was filled with great joy as he urged the bishop to come home with him and "see my children." Well, the bishop thought, this man is a fast worker, to have a home and children so soon! He agreed to go with him and together they walked down the street. The man stopped and bought several sacks of candy "for my children," and when they at last arrived in front of a large house with a spacious lawn filled with laughing children, the bishop began to understand. As their foster father distributed the candy, the children clung to his coat and hugged his legs. Looking up with smiling face, he said to Bishop Chen: "You see, I have learned what is meant by the way of the cross. Though I lost my home and my family, I have another home and all these wonderful homeless children to love and to live for!"

Illustrations are plentiful of the way in which an acceptance of the love of God fills the heart with good will toward man. There is ample evidence that forgiveness is not an impractical luxury, or an impossible demand, but rather the blessed overflow of Christ's love in our own lives.

Such compassionate forgiveness came to Stephen as he knelt, "gazed into heaven and saw the glory of God, and Jesus . . ." (Acts 7:55-60). In the light of this mighty overflowing love of God in Christ, he could follow his Master in the prayer "Lord, do not hold this sin against them."

It is not human forgiveness that we give, but the forgiveness of God. Our own forgiveness is contingent on our willingness to give to others what has been given to us. "Forgive us our debts, *as we also have forgiven* our debtors." "In making up His accounts with us," says St. Teresa, "God is never strict but always generous. However great our debt, He thinks it a small matter if through it He can gain us." He does not gain us, however, until we are willing to let his love pour through us to others!

What a blessed reality is forgiving love! How quickly it can break up the hardened soil of our own hearts: receiving from God and giving to others!

Forgiveness is not an effort, a stern duty; but the delighted overflow of a compassionate, self-oblivious charity. It is the joy with which, after long exhausting search, the tiresome sheep is found, the lost coin hunted down; the delight of the father receiving safe and sound the worthless son who has disgraced the family name, wasted the family money, and only remembered family affection when all other resources failed. Even here, forgiveness means music and dancing; no hint of disapproval, all memory of folly and ingratitude drowned in love. Mercy and grimness cannot live together.[21]

The end of the matter is this: In combating evil we must love as God loves, with a steady, unrelenting intolerance of wrong no matter in what form it appears, and we must take "the longest stride of soul men ever took" in order to remove or cancel it. We must also love as God loves in "a multitude of tender mercies" toward the blind and foolish wrongdoers, that wherever possible we may open the door to them for the love that never gives up. It is life's most priceless privilege to share in this cosmic, redemptive love and to be a small channel of His mighty grace!

[21] Evelyn Underhill, *Abba* (New York: Longmans, Green and Co., 1940), p. 70.

VII. Finding Peace
and Fortitude Through Love

"Peace! Peace! This I desire above everything else. Just give me peace and I don't care what happens!"

This exclamation describes the mood of a great many people today, not only in Europe and in the Middle and Far East but in America. It expresses the sense of futility of those whose compassionate concern has burned out in the fires of struggle and frustration. Tired of war, desiring union with others, longing for love, they are disappointed, beaten, confused. Now if they can't have love, they want peace of mind or at least a negative peace in their environment which is the absence of conflict.

There are other wars, of course, than those between nations and groups. A pathetic scene immediately comes to my mind: an exhausted mother with three crying children hanging onto her dress. She lives in a constant state of tension and conflict with a husband who is a "bear," who comes home either drunk or irritable and unbearable. Her life is a constant battleground. She says to me, "Is there any way I can find peace?"

What she and all the rest of us really need, however, is not the mere cessation of conflict, the absence of open war, of struggle and tension, as much as we may desire it. For this may be and often is the peace of death, or, at best, a vegetable peace in which we cease to grow and live as human beings. One poet has put our wistful desires in these words: "Let me grow softly as the grasses grow!"

But we are not grass; we are men and women and children —human beings called to live as the sons and daughters of God. We are responsible. We have freedom, and we cannot avoid the struggle or escape the tensions. To do so is to die. Such false peace is like the good feeling that comes after you quit hitting your finger and the pain ceases. It feels good at the time, but what do you then do with your finger?

The only kind of peace that is healthy and desirable is that which accompanies real love as a fruit of the Spirit (Gal. 5:21). It comes as the gift of God's love, even in the middle of conflict and tensions, at the height of human striving: the peace of God in the soul fitting us to live and grow!

> Peace does not mean the end of all our striving,
> Joy does not mean the drying of our tears;
> Peace is the power that comes to souls arriving
> Up to the light where God Himself appears.[1]

This is the kind of peace Jeremiah and Ezekiel and Jesus were talking about. "Shalom," the Hebrew word for peace, means much more than the absence of war; it means the power to live harmoniously and with true spiritual prosperity even in the midst of conflict—and what is just as important, the ability to be a peacemaker. "Blessed are the peacemakers, for they shall be called sons of God" is the beatitude of Jesus which describes the result in our human relations of the deep peace which Jesus offered to all those who would follow him as sons of the heavenly Father.

The union of peace with love is the distinctive contribution of Christian faith and belongs increasingly to those who learn to accept themselves and their fellows in the steadfast Love that endures forever!

What Jesus and the New Testament writers meant by peace is really that calm fortitude which the ancient Greeks and Romans so admired, but with a plus which they could only dimly grasp. The very first cardinal virtue, according to them, was called *fortitude:*

[1] Excerpt from "The Suffering God" (pages 12-14) in *The Sorrows of God* and Other Poems by G. A. Studdert-Kennedy. Copyright, 1924, by Harper & Row, Publishers, Inc. Renewed 1952 by Emily Studdert-Kennedy. By permission of the publisher.

firmness of mind in meeting dangers and adversities, resolute endurance, staying power. Christian peace with Christlike love, however, is much more than grit and pluck, which could easily become a naïve acceptance of evil situations that should never be accepted and that result in disastrous hurt to others and, in the long run, to our own well-being. A loving peace within us is the very foundation upon which either a wise tolerance or a helpful intolerance can be had, and at the same time an inner calmness which keeps us from going to pieces under the strain.

Obviously this is the kind of peace we need. Not the peace of a vegetable slowly rotting, or the peace of an animal sleeping in the sunshine, but the peace of a son or daughter of God arriving up to the light where God himself appears! In this chapter I shall seek to show the age-old folly of peace without love, which I am calling peace at any price; and the perennial miracle of a creative, redemptive peace with fortitude that forever springs from real love.

Peace Without Love Is Too Costly

The most frequently used way of finding peace is the old, sad way of peace at any price. Ultimately this kind of peace will prove to be false and destructive—for us as individuals as well as for the race—and therefore too costly, for it is a denial of and an escape from strong, wise giving-love.

When It Is an Escape from Struggle

Peace at any price is too costly when it is merely an escape from conflict and struggle. The modern peace-of-mind cult that puts peace of mind as the major goal in life is particularly appealing to those who are so tired or bored or disgusted with life that they just want to lie down. The recent flood of books on "How to Relax," "How to Quit Worrying" are symptoms of a weary generation which has pretty largely lost the great meaning and challenge of life. Many times we who seek peace need to do anything but run away and relax! We all need to know *How to Worry Successfully,*[2] as one writer ironically titles his book.

It is revealing to note the enormous amount of money and energy that is spent by millions of Americans in the quest for peace. A large part of the cost of alcoholic beverages, which runs up into the billions of dollars—several times as much as is spent on churches and education put together—is spent because alcohol is an anesthetic. It deadens one's nerves, puts one's mind and conscience to sleep, makes one lie down even when standing up or driving a car. There were 40,000 people killed in automobile accidents in one year, and a traffic expert will tell you that many of them lost their lives because someone was lying down at the wheel. This is what makes alcohol so lethal. It is the perverted fortitude of folly!

The alcoholic peace is a pseudo peace that is too costly—for when the effects wear off after the accident has happened, after the silly words are said and the foolish deeds are done, or even after the body and mind have been put completely to sleep, one is right back where he started, but with an even greater sense of guilt and inadequacy than before. He has less grit and guts to stand life than ever. The same is true of the excessive use of narcotics and tranquilizing drugs (fifteen tons of sleeping pills in one year is a lot of pills!), and even of tobacco, through which many seek to escape in a haze of smoke. Certainly the overwhelming increase in the quest for entertainment stems from the same need to escape, "to relax and forget ourselves."

Now it is surely good and necessary that we have times when we relax and forget ourselves. And there are times when our physical bodies require the aid of sleeping pills and tranquillizers. Laughter and fun are good medicine, but only if this forgetting of ourselves in entertainment is not a substitute for real peace of soul. Recreation that re-creates is good, giving us alternating periods of rest and relaxation, fitting us to go back to the struggle; but as an escape from the issues that cause our conflict, it is entirely too costly.

[2] David Seabury (Boston: Little, Brown and Co., 1938).

Even the reading of books, whether "whodunits" or "highbrow books" of philosophy and literature, is too costly if this is our way of attempting to escape conflict by shutting ourselves up in an ivory tower.

And what shall we say of a religion, private or social, that seeks primarily to use our faith in God as an anodyne, an opiate to deaden our nerves, while we excuse or forget the suffering and need all about us? Such faith is as dangerous as alcohol or narcotics. It deadens our spirits and dulls our consciences until the storm strikes and we are helpless. I do not know of any more helpless person than one who for years has used his religion as an escape and then suddenly faces suffering and trouble from which he cannot escape, and finds that his religion of relaxation is useless. How often have I heard from such persons the despairing words, "God has let me down!"

The same may be true of a society or a nation. From ancient Greece and Rome to our modern world, the motto of every dying civilization has been "peace at any price." Rome's fall began when her aristocracy decided to buy the support of the plebeian crowds with shiploads of wheat doled out to them rather than to merit their support through the more difficult and costly way of mutual responsibility and co-operation.

Our human tragedy is that this all-out effort for peace does not bring real peace. Instead, too often, as Jeremiah put it:

> We looked for peace, but no good came,
> for a time of healing, but behold, terror.

The writings of Jeremiah and Ezekiel and the other prophets are filled with warnings to the leaders of Israel who had grown soft and hoped to stave off trouble by bribing the nations surrounding them. Listen to the stinging rebuke given to these false leaders who could encourage and take advantage of this desire in their fellows to escape conflict:

They have misled my people, saying, "Peace," when there is no peace; and because, when the people build a wall, these prophets daub it with whitewash; say to those who daub it with whitewash that it shall fall! There will be a deluge of rain . . . and a stormy wind break out; and when the wall falls, will it not be said to you, "Where is the daubing with which you daubed it?" (Ezekiel 13:10-12.)

Anything that keeps us from seeing and meeting the real issues with the concern of a wise love, that prevents us from facing the struggle and finding God's will in it, is whitewash, daubing the cracks. Even positive thinking or prayer becomes the deadliest whitewash of all when used to daub the cracks of our houses of ease and security and pleasure as we shut out the call of love to help bear or remove the burdens of our fellows. Amos' stinging rebuke to those in his day who sought peace without love applies to every day, certainly to ours:

Woe to those who are at ease in Zion, . . . who feel secure on the mountain of Samaria. . . . Woe to those who lie upon beds of ivory, and stretch themselves upon their couches, . . . who sing idle songs to the sound of the harp, . . . who drink wine in bowls, . . . but are not grieved over the ruin of Joseph! (6:1-6.)

The physical comforts of human life and the solace of prayer and worship become deadly evils when they are used as whitewash to support a home of false peace where we lose our concern for the ruin of Joseph! Such peace is too expensive!

The frequent use of piety as an escape from the call of love was obvious to Karl Marx. Not having seen the kind of piety that produces loving concern, he proclaimed what has become an axiom for all Marxist Communists around the world, "Religion is an opiate to the people." The pitiable thing is that the Christianity Karl Marx knew was so vitiated by self-righteous goodness that there was little real love left!

136

When It Is Built on Immoral Foundations

Peace at any price is too costly when it is built on a false foundation, contrary to God's moral and spiritual law. This is true for a world, a nation, a home, or an individual. Cried the Lord through Isaiah:

> O that you had harkened to my commandments!
> Then your peace would have been like a river,
> and your righteousness like the waves of the sea.
>
> . . . .
>
> "There is no peace," says the Lord, "for the wicked."

No peace to the wicked? But who are the wicked? Not we or our friends or our associates, certainly; only our enemies, or the racketeers or dissolute persons, or Communists! It is hard for any one of us to recognize the wickedness of our own blind, perverse refusal to see facts—facts which might cause us inconvenience and disturb our tranquillity. Call them by what name you will, the wicked are those who refuse to see the moral and spiritual requirements for genuine peace; or, to put it differently, who want peace but not the sacrifices and moral stamina that are the foundations of real peace.

There can be no peace between nations except through moral law to which the leaders of the nations and the people give, not lip service, but genuine respect and obedience. The Ten Commandments, and the greater law of love for God and man which includes all ten, were graven not merely on tablets of stone, but on the tablets of humanity. There is no peace or freedom except through love and respect for the law and the truth about our relations to God and our fellows.

When any worthy peace comes, it is on the foundations of truth and love. Even the military and political leaders of our nation declare this to be so. For this we should be thankful. Only, they and we must not be fooled into thinking that by *talking about* truth and love and adding the phrase *under God* to our pledge of al-

137

legiance to the flag, we do thereby have truth and love and are truly living under God. Nevertheless, it is hopeful when our leaders recognize, as did General Douglas MacArthur at the signing of the Japanese peace treaty in Tokyo Harbor, that "if we do not now devise some greater and more equitable system, Armageddon will be at our door." Or, in the words of another general, Dwight D. Eisenhower, "Unless America experiences a moral and spiritual regeneration, we shall all disappear in the dust of an atomic explosion." Or, again, in the words of Ralph Bunche, an effective troubleshooter for the United Nations:

Now, people in society can live together only if their relations are governed by some recognition, however imperfect, of moral law and mutual respect. The nations of the world, which make up the international community, must be similarly governed in their relationships or there will be international chaos on a scale beggaring description and with consequences, in this atomic era, too forbidding to contemplate.[3]

The deciding question, however, is not how we talk but how we do!

We simply cannot have that peace among races which is so necessary in this kind of world, whether in South Africa, or Asia, or America, except through understanding love that goes deeper than physical or cultural differences and establishes a relationship of justice and mutual respect and co-operation. For real love knows no color line in the human family. Anything less than this, no matter what it is called, is whitewash, and the relationship will fall, "and a stormy wind break out; and when the wall falls, will it not be said to you, 'Where is the daubing with which you daubed it?' " (Ezek. 13:11-12).

How often has every marriage counselor seen the whitewashed relationships between husband and wife fall with a resounding thud. One or the other attempts to buy peace, merely to go along, to bribe the other, or to force peace on his or her own terms. Sometimes the whitewash is a sentimental righteousness by which "the

[3] See "Toward Peace and Freedom," *The Christian Century*, April 22, 1953.

virtuous one" seeks to dominate the other (of course, "in the name of God"). But, whatever method we use, this self-centered daubing of our walls of peace cannot keep them from falling, because we have left out the strong foundation of wise love with its mutual respect and trustful co-operation.

Carl Sandburg, writing during the time of false peace before the Second World War, gave this warning to all who seek peace without love. His satirical words burn with the truth which we do not like to see:

So what? So we must be calm, collected, easy, facing the next war,
And we can remember the man sitting on a red hot stove as he sniffed the air, "Is something burning?"
Or the Kansas farmer, "We asked the cyclone to go around our barn but it didn't hear us."
Or we can turn to the Books and take a looksee and then take a cry or a laugh, as it pleases.
They say, do the Books: Begin your war and it becomes something else than you saw before it began—it runs longer or shorter than planned, it comes out like nobody running it expected, ending with both sides saying, "We are surprised at what happened!" [4]

Well, now there is no longer any element of surprise as to what will happen as far as our international peace is concerned. It is terribly clear. Fear of the hydrogen or cobalt bomb, within itself, is no guarantee that we will have peace. Peace is not made by the desire to escape conflict or destruction. The threats of atomic destruction may be a deterrent to open war, but peace itself will come only by open-minded obedience to the Truth.

When It Is Contrary to the Spirit of Christlike Love

Peace at any price is too costly when it is contrary to the spirit of Christlike love, which is the heart and core of God's moral law.

[4] "The Unknown War," from *Complete Poems*, copyright, 1950, by Carl Sandburg. Reprinted by permission of Harcourt, Brace and Company, Inc.

This is the conclusion of the whole matter. This was the meaning behind Jesus' words, "Do not think that I have come to bring peace on earth; I have not come to bring peace, but a sword. For I have come to set a man against his father, and a daughter against her mother . . . ; and a man's foes will be those of his own household" (Matt. 10:34-35). That is, to paraphrase his meaning, "I did not come to bring a false peace; as long as there is wrong against any member of the family, there can be no peace in that family; and my spirit in any person will keep that person from accepting a false peace where love is denied."

Remember the words of Theodore Roosevelt, back in 1910, as he received the Nobel Peace Prize:

We must bear in mind that the great end in view is righteousness, justice as between man and man, nation and nation, the chance to lead our lives on a somewhat higher level, with a broader spirit of brotherly love for one another. . . . Peace is generally good in itself, but it is never the highest good unless it comes as a handmaid of righteousness and it becomes a very evil thing if it serves merely as a mask for cowardice or sloth, or as an instrument to further the ends of despotism and anarchy!

For truly, "The only good thing is a good will." Peace is a positive evil without the good will. If to protect myself from conflict and trouble I reject the highest good for my home or people or nation or world, I am guilty of damnable evil. I have sinned against love. "Peace at any price" is a deadly evil.

Peace with Fortitude a Result of Love

Peace with fortitude serves only as the result of my faith in God by which I am able to fulfill the law of love!

Such peace is not passive, but the "ordered, harmonious function of the whole person." It is a creative, loving peace which is the gift of God by which I am lifted to a new perspective. Even in the midst of conflict, I am able to see those who oppose me as human beings like myself, children of God, and to see in my struggle a greater possibility than winning or losing what I am after. The peace I then have is not the tranquillity of death or of a desert isle. It is the deeper and more genuine tranquillity of an unshakable confidence in the loving resources of God at my disposal, and the assurance that in their use I can do the best things even in the worst times. Then I will have "the patience to see the things I cannot change; the courage to change what I can, and the wisdom to know the difference!" This is Christian peace and fortitude which can never be evil.

Such peace must begin *within me.* Some people are obsessed with the desire to wipe out the faults of others. "We could have peace if everyone would do as I say"—yes, but it would be a false peace, the opposite of freedom. Creative peace in the midst of conflict must begin first in me!

Remember those beautiful words in Edna St. Vincent Millay's *Conversation at Midnight,* in which the priest says:

There is no peace on earth today save the peace in the heart
At home with God. From that sure habitation
The heart looks forth upon the sorrows of the savage world
And pities them, and ministers to them; but is not implicated [drawn
  into their falseness].
All else has failed, as it must always fail.
No man can be at peace with his neighbour who is not at peace
With himself; the troubled mind is a trouble maker![5]

Yes, the troubled mind is the troublemaker. Only he who is at peace with himself can help bring peace around him. There is no peace without a great love, and where there is a great love there will be a genuine peace in spite of the struggles and conflicts.

It is significant that Jesus spoke most about peace, not during the sunny days in Galilee when everything was going well, but as he approached the dark hour of the cross. Then it was he said: "Peace I leave with you; my peace I give to you; not as the world gives. . . . Let not your hearts be troubled, neither let them be afraid." (John 14:27.) "I give the deep, enduring, tranquil peace, the inward quiet of acceptance, the mind stayed on God ready for anything because anchored on His Eternal Reality—indifferent to its own risks, comforts or achievements, sunk in the great movement of His life," [6] thus Evelyn Underhill paraphrases Jesus' words. Surely this was the peace possessed by Jesus: peace that was not apathy in the presence of the world's sorrow and pain, but peace that was the calm, sure confidence that determined to do anything necessary, even to taking the cross, in order that all men might meet the world's pain and evil with victory. It was the peace with a great price, the price of the cross. Hence, we speak of it as "the peace of the cross," perhaps the most contradictory use of words we can imagine, but in Jesus' experience, and that of many who have followed him, gloriously true. And in this peace there is joy and fortitude, strength and freedom. The peace of the cross is a peace "of absolute acceptance, utter abandonment to God—a peace inseparable from sacrifice." [7]

Such peace is possible to every one of us. Listen to the testimonies of great spirits, known and unknown, in every age who have received this gift from God. From Paul and Silas singing in prison at midnight, to Kagawa thrown into prison, or threatened by mobs, or faced with blindness due to an eye disease, keeping "the Jewel of peace" hidden in his soul!

Hear the tesimony of Cardinal Mercier, who, along with King Albert I of Belgium, brought strength and hope to the besieged Belgians during World War I. He wrote:

[6] *The Fruits of the Spirit* (New York: Longmans, Green and Co., 1942), pp. 12-13.
[7] *Ibid.*

142

Whether in the years of peace or the years of war, whether in poverty or prosperity, whether in failure or success, never have I failed to feel deep down in my heart a sense of tranquility, confidence and peace. . . . I must tell you the secret of Christian serenity. It lies in giving yourself confidently to the goodness of the Lord.[8]

I know a woman whose husband at one time was an alcoholic, and, whether drunk or sober, was a devil to live with. When I first knew her, she had adopted the course of peace at any price. She babied him, nagged him, fought him, protected him, drank with him, kept him from feeling the full results of his running from life; but through it all she hated him, and her resentment flared up at times. She was continually vacillating between appeasement and conflict. He only fought her the more and drank and cursed the more. One day she discovered she had not really loved him for years. Oh, she had clung to him from pride, from a desire for security and the memory of the love they once had; but she no longer loved him. She was really more concerned about her own feelings than about him.

Then she began to get an insight into her own miseries and self-doubtings and to surrender them to the forgiving love of God. She began to live with an outgoing love that, though still concerned about her own security and well-being, was trusting *that* to God and was determined to do everything she could to save her husband. She looked upon him with new eyes. She went to meetings of Alcoholics Anonymous and persuaded him to go. She loved him with a tender kindness he had missed before. She no longer used sex as a weapon to show her resentment. She loved him more, and more completely—not the false self that he hated and that God hated—but the true person that God loved and that he really could be.

She discovered for the first time a deep peace of mind, a real

---

[8] Quoted in *The Whole Armor of God* by Ralph Sockman (Nashville: Abingdon Press, 1955), p. 51.

fortitude, a staying power that was not negative: she found out she could help him. Today both of them are on the way to being made whole, because she surrendered her "peace at any price" and found the true peace that begins in love and ends in genuine fortitude! Yes, there was a cross in it, just as there always is when we love deeply; but the joy of their restored relationship and new life far outweighed the cost, just as it always does.

Such peace can be yours when your heart is at home with God. Do not run away from the conflict inside you, working only to remove the conflict in others. Refuse to anesthetize your soul. Enjoy rest, recreation, fun, but let it be a rest and not an escape.

Accept the things you cannot change. Quit fighting the facts of your situation. This may mean accepting many minor or even major faults in those with whom you live which you would like to change, but which when attacked simply cause you and them to lose other things far more precious.

Change the things that you can change. With courageous humility, renounce all "holier than thou" or superior attitudes. Approach the things that are evil in your situation, whether personal, community, church, national, or world-wide, with an outgoing, confident giving-love. Work *with* others, on their level, not *against* them from a higher level. Your symptoms of sin may be different from theirs but your sin is the same: prideful self-love seeking to save your false self-image. Recognize this and there will be no "stooping over" to help. Share your experiences with those you seek to help, remembering that the change must come from the inside. It is they, through God's help, that make the change, not you; and all your nagging, fighting, protesting will simply harden the clay, not soften it. When, as indicated in the preceding chapter, there has to be conflict, let it be with love that is ready to heal the wounds and to forgive.

Learn to trust the infinite resources of God within you. Peace is a gift; learn to take it. This is one gift we do not grab, or clutch, or fight and struggle over. Like rest given to us as we sleep, so peace is given to us when we cease to demand it and give ourselves trustingly to the goodness of the Lord.

Learn to love if you would know true peace! This is the best wisdom of all. "There is no fear in love, but perfect love casts out fear." (I John 4:18.) I shall not forget the story told by Gregory Vlastos, a young Canadian Christian who spent several months in Spain during the revolution preceding World War II. On his return, he described for some of us the experience he had had during his first bombing. He and his companions rushed to a bomb cellar, where they waited as the bombs fell screaming one after another, dangerously near. Perspiration was streaming down his face. He was afraid, to put it mildly—terror-stricken indeed! "Then I looked to one corner of the cellar and saw a Spanish mother calmly and quietly telling a story to her children who gathered around her trustingly. I asked her how she could be so calm and unafraid under such conditions. She answered that she didn't have time to be afraid, she must keep her children from fear! Then I remembered the words in First John, 'Perfect love casts out fear!'"

And so it does! Try this the next time you find yourself irritated and upset, anxious and distraught, your peace gone; find someone in your family or your office or community who is in need of your encouragement and help. Or better, give yourself to the service of a great concern, not for a few minutes but for life, and you will find peace which nothing can shake. Giving-love rooted in the Divine Peace takes away fear.

Esther, one of Lloyd Douglas' most beautiful characters in *The Big Fisherman*, was listening intently as Jesus spoke to the crowd. He was speaking about the blessed abundant life:

. . . freed of fear and foreboding, freed of frets and suspicions, freed of the sweating greed for perishable things. This was the life he offered, a life of enduring peace in the midst of the world's clamors and confusions. . . .

The Carpenter's peace invited her spirit. . . . Anyone could possess it [he said]. It was to be had for the asking, but one must seek for it, work for it; and, if need be, suffer for it. It was like living water, drawn from an everflowing spring. Once you had tasted of it, you would never again be satisfied without it. It might cost you many a sacrifice, but it would be worth the price.... [It was] the peace-power of the Father's Kingdom.[9]

Yes, such creative, loving peace is costly. It costs the sacrifice of all evasions, of all demands on life and God. It costs the surrender of all our secret longings for self-exaltation. It requires the giving of oneself to the splendor of God's truth about oneself and the world, willing to be used for the kingdom of God for all. This peace-power of the Kingdom is available to all who will accept it in daily, hourly trust. To all who will take up their crosses and follow Him, it is a blessed gift.

[9](Boston: Houghton Mifflin Co., 1948), p. 217. Used by permission.

VIII. The Just and the Loving

We will either love and live or, failing to love, we will die to the beauty and meaning of life; and the love we need is strong, affirmative, Christlike. On this most of us are agreed. But who can love in such gracious strength and wisdom?

Who can think and act in the joyous freedom of a courageous humility, seeing and responding to the real facts of the situation?

Who can give as a wise spendthrift the prodigal gifts of love without which life is barren, ugly, and meaningless?

Who can delight in obedience to duty and give himself in glad service to his fellows as part of the redemptive force of the new age?

Who can be blessedly intolerant, as well as tolerant, in the right spirit and at the right time and place?

Who can possess creative, constructive peace and fortitude, joined to a loving concern, even in the midst of conflict?

And in this concluding chapter, we ask, Who can be just in his dealings with others and with himself, his own body and time and life?

These are truly our most pressing questions.

Here there are many pessimists. Such love is only a freak accident, they say. It does not belong in the hopes of the average person —maybe for a few mountain-peak persons but not for me or you. Therefore, there is only one way to keep any measure of goodness or justice in human life and that is through the force of law. Take the law away and goodness disappears. Our only hope is in the acceptance and enforcement of the right laws, whether in the home or the community or nation or world. Certainly there is some truth in this position.

The Power of the Law

There are some things that the law can do that wouldn't get done otherwise. Without law, civilization in its broadest aspects—peaceful industry, commerce, culture, education, homelife—would not be possible. Where would we be in this old world today without laws—the laws of traffic, safety, health, the penal and moral laws accepted by the customs of the community and the consciences of the people? Legal and penal justice have their place.

Suppose the traffic laws were repealed and every man were on his own? Every man would find himself colliding with another; life would become a nightmare, and we would immediately call a citizens' committee to formulate some new laws. As Bishop Francis J. McConnell used to say, "There must be traffic officers even in heaven to keep the saints from too many collisions!" It is even well that people keep laws for fear of being caught. Bishop F. Gerald Ensley said: "I do not think there are many saints in this life who have attained such a high state of grace that a vision of a traffic officer makes any difference whatsoever to their driving." He urged us not to forget that it is not only the doctors and nurses and educators and ministers who are building the kingdom but also the lawyers "who spell out humanity's moral insights into the statute and who cast a mantle of protection about humanity's noblest interests." [1] Yes, we ought to appreciate law and those who make and uphold it.

And certainly public opinion is a powerful influence for good. Remove the force of public opinion and every one of us would have to sleep with a gun under his pillow. There are many people who would do all kinds of evil, selfish, greedy things if they thought they could get away with it.

Thank God for the law, not only external but within. Paul said: "The law was our schoolmaster to bring us unto Christ." (Gal. 3:24 K.J.V.) He was talking not only of the law as given to Moses but of the moral law in our own consciences, the sense of oughtness

[1] From an address at the General Conference of The Methodist Church, April 30, 1956.

148

that separates us from the animal. "Two things fill the mind with ever new and increasing wonder and awe," wrote Kant, "the starry heavens above me and the moral law within me."

The Inadequacy of the Law

And yet, there are some things which the law cannot do. However just and right the laws, whether of God or of men, whether in our own conscience or in public opinion, they can never produce true goodness and justice, real virtue, forgiveness, an understanding mind, a heart of love, for the simple reason that such goodness cannot be forced. We are free beings with wills capable of choosing our own values and goals. You can lead a horse to water. You cannot make him drink, although as W. E. Hocking used to say, "Sometimes when the horse gets to the water, he decides he wants to drink." You can force external obedience, your own or others. You can't make anyone like it or put his heart in it. This is the difference between slave and free labor—in giving out of a heart of love that knows no burden and in being driven to comply with law while remaining always ready to turn the other way when the chance comes. Outward compliance with the law is no guarantee that our acts will be good for us or in the long run good for others. True goodness is the result of free, spontaneous giving-love.

So we are right back where we started: How do we get this strong, courageous, wise love? The Christian answer is unequivocal: Such love comes only through the overflow of God's grace spilling out from our lives to others. It is thus only that you really do good, just as your own lives have been the recipients of grace which has spilled over on you from other peoples' lives. "What the law could not do in that it was weak, God did and continues to do, sending his own Son." (paraphrase, Rom. 8:3.)

Self-Righteousness Always Fails

In each of the preceding chapters, I have given some indications of the meaning of this central truth of the Christian faith. In this

149

chapter, let us look more closely at the fact that our self-centered attempts to secure the good, lovely, and just in our own lives and in our world always end in failure. Without agape love our justice becomes injustice and our righteousness becomes unrighteous and evil. In fact, without real love there can be no true justice. I will give some illustrations of the way in which such virtues as chastity, temperance, abstinence, and obedience to social or moral laws may become deadly and hurtful rather than blessed and helpful. I will seek to make clear the way of divine grace, which transforms these and all other self-righteous virtues into expressions of the love that never fails!

The false ways by which men have sought true goodness could be summarized in one word, *self-righteousness.* "Being ignorant of the righteousness that comes from God, and seeking to establish their own," says Paul, "they do not submit to God's righteousness." (Rom. 10:3.) What they do in the name of justice, therefore, turns out to be unjust to themselves and others.

There are many kinds of self-righteousness. There is, for instance, honor of a certain kind even among thieves, a code of right and wrong (not conventional, of course) by which they preserve their own self-respect and the regard of their partners in crime and by which they justify their thievery. According to the code of thieves, it is all right to steal from the rich and prosperous so long as you are charitable to your fellow thieves and don't "rat" on them.

This is one concept, at least, that thieves and decent, respectable, "moral" men and women have in common. Such codes of right and wrong enable us to hold our heads up, to consider ourselves good thieves or butchers, bakers or candlestick makers; and by adhering to the codes, we live together with some harmony.

There is much to be said for this method of producing virtue. Without law-abiding citizens we would have complete anarchy, an impossible situation even among thieves! Civilization itself would surely be impossible, for it has been built very largely on the basis of human experience through countless centuries—experience that has been codified into a system of law and order. This system has come to be respected by a large majority of the people. The great jurist Oliver Wendell Holmes was fond of saying that law is crystallized public necessity. "The life of the law has not been logic; it has been experience—the felt necessities of the time." [2]

The Ten Commandments, as given by God to Moses, were not all the inspiration of the moment, or even of the forty days and nights on Mt. Sinai. They were the distilled wisdom of centuries, as indicated by the fact that most of them are found in other ancient codes, such as the code of Hammurabi of the Babylonians. There has been growth in the law. Just as the Old Testament law of "an eye for an eye, and a tooth for a tooth" was a great advance over the old law permitting unlimited revenge for an injury, so Jesus' insight obviously is more realistic, "I say to you, Love your enemy and pray for those who persecute you" (Matt. 5:44). Jesus recognized the value of the law, "I have come not to abolish [the law] but to fulfil [it]" (Matt. 5:17).

Now certainly self-righteous obedience to laws is better than complete lawlessness, but it is far from being sufficient. One reason is in the nature of self-righteousness. For self-righteousness is the arbitrary picking of certain laws I choose to obey, whether moral or legal, while excusing myself for letting other laws go unrecognized and unobeyed. "We damn the sins we have no mind to," said Oscar Wilde, but the sins we do have a mind to we don't think bad at all!

The great trouble with trying to achieve goodness and justice through such self-righteous legalism (keeping the letter of the law as I see it) is that it is too easily a means of hiding from myself my lack of giving-love, the one desperately needed power in our lives and world. The strict, meticulous observance of moral laws, even those I claim as God's laws, may contain such a large element

[2] Catherine Drinker Bowen, *Yankee from Olympus* (Boston: Little, Brown and Co., 1944), p. 275.

of pride and self-sufficiency that through self-deception I become immune to the love of God and thereby unable to love my fellows in true sincerity and in the right perspective.

This was the wrong in the legalism of the Pharisees of Jesus' day. Jesus knew the law of the Sabbath was good in principle. He reverenced the Sabbath as a day of rest and worship which man needed. "The Sabbath was made for man," he said. But he also knew that the strict Sabbatarianism of the scribes and Pharisees turned the law around and made human needs subordinate to the law of the Sabbath. What began as good became unjust because it was injurious to man. One of the hundreds of laws on Sabbath observance declared that one must not travel from one's residence more than two thousand cubits on the Sabbath. The Pharisees got around this law by sending their servants, the day before, to deposit at intervals of two thousand cubits some valueless article such as an old sandal, a broken pot, or a bit of cast-off clothing. The next day the law-abiding master could travel ten miles without getting more than two thousand cubits from his residence! Jesus knew their "righteousness" was a deadly hypocrisy. It served only to elevate the ego of those who practiced it and had nothing to do with love of God and man, which is true religion.

Legalism did not end with the Pharisees. Even in the days of the Reformation, whose leaders were trying to get away from the legalism of the Roman Church, preaching "justification by faith and not by works," there were attempts to regulate conduct and produce justice and goodness by force. In the account of John Calvin's Court of Consistorial Discipline, which followed the Genevese citizen from his cradle to his grave, there is

a strange and mournful record, with ludicrous lights crossing it here and there. A man hearing an ass bray, and saying jestingly, "Il chante un beau psaume" (He's chanting a lovely psalm), is sentenced to temporary banishment from the city. A young girl in church singing the words of a song to a psalm tune is ordered to be whipped by her parents. A man, for swearing "by the body and blood of Christ," is condemned to be fined and to sit in the public square in stocks. A child, for having struck her parents, was beheaded in 1568. This consistorial discipline is declared to be "the yoke of Christ" . . . the [whole thing] is carried back to scripture and presumed to rest upon express Divine command.[3]

Among the Puritans in the early days of our own country, the attempt to live by rule, to place law before love, was productive of much injury and wrong. Somewhere in the Bible the Puritan could find a rule for any given situation and this rule he followed meticulously. *The Scarlet Letter* by Hawthorne dramatically portrays this tragedy in the persecution that was heaped upon an erring young couple. They had sinned and broken the law, it is true, but there was no mercy, no second chance. Their whole lives were ruined by this unloving self-righteousness. Again, the law had become superior to love.

The difficulty with all moral codes is that human nature cannot be thrust into a strait jacket of rules and laws. Every moral code is made to be broken. "Good men break it from above and bad men from below," as George A. Buttrick points out. This was the reason Jesus was crucified between two thieves: all three had broken the moral code. The word "ethics" comes from the Greek word meaning "stable." Mankind has always desired to get right and wrong completely identified and secure like a horse in a stable! We would all like to have a safe set of rules to live by which always remain the same so that we need never bother about thinking. How comfortable it would be to live in a world where we could just turn to rule No. 569 or obey law No. IV and always be right! But unfortunately—or rather fortunately for our growth in character—this is not that kind of world. As the child's verse puts it:

> The other night, from cares exempt,
> I slept—and what d'you think I dreamt?

[3] Tulloch, *op. cit.*, pp. 207-8.

> I dreamt that somehow I had come
> To dwell in Topsy-Turveydom!—
> Where vice is virtue—virtue, vice:
> Where nice is nasty—nasty, nice.[4]

Topsy-turveydom is a good name for our human relationships, wherein there is never a nice, neat description of vice and virtue, of good and evil. You can't live by the book of rules, and when you try your justice and righteousness turn into injustice and unrighteousness, and your virtues into vices.

Recall the biting words of Bernard Shaw's Don Juan in *Man and Superman*. An old woman joins Don Juan in hell.

"Where are we?" she asks in her confusion.

"In hell," he answers.

Indignantly, she asks him how *she* could possibly be in hell, she a lady of virtue and honor, a "faithful daughter of the Church," with a whole sheaf of good deeds to recommend her. Oh, she had not been perfect, but who has?

"I am here: in hell, you tell me: that is the reward of duty. Is there justice in heaven?"

Don Juan answers: "You will be welcome in hell, Señora. Hell is the home of honor, duty, justice, and the rest of the seven deadly virtues. All the wickedness on earth is done in their name: where else but in hell should they have their reward?" [5]

Surely history and experience bear out the insight of these lines: even our virtues become deadly when we hold them as proofs of our superiority or as insurance against insecurity. "Unless your righteousness exceeds that of the scribes and Pharisees, you will never enter the kingdom of Heaven," thus Jesus puts our human situation. The scribes and Pharisees were legalists attempting to get everybody to subscribe to their moral code, but without the strong, wise giving-love that could have helped them to see what was truly right and just. As a result of their blindness, the supreme

[4] Sir William Schwenck Gilbert. "My Dream."

[5] Used by permission of The Society of Authors on behalf of the Bernard Shaw Estate.

illustration of the tragedy and cruelty of self-righteous legalism is Christ on the cross! "So in every age, the vices, crimes, and sins of society are [often] the root and overflow of its virtues."

Before we become too horrified at the legalistic extremes of the past, let us look at our own lives in these so-called enlightened times. Consider, for example, how the moral problems of chastity, temperance and abstinence, and divorce can be solved only by real love. The attempt to solve these problems on any other basis has resulted in self-righteous pride, cruelty without mercy to those who broke the rules, and sickness in the minds of those who kept them.

Three Moral Problems Only Love Can Solve

Chastity

To say that observing the rules of chastity is not enough is not to minimize the moral laws of sex and of the health of our bodies and minds. It is to recognize the point Jesus made clear: adultery is not confined to the overt act. The right use of the sexual drive and of bodily appetite cannot, however, be guaranteed by law of any kind.

The law must be fulfilled by love, which alone can enable one to treat his body or the body of another with justice. Now justice is simply the quality or principle of rectitude or right dealing of men with themselves and with others. When justice is done to a meal, it is eaten with proper zest and appreciation. Justice in any situation is the best possible solution for all involved. Justice in regard to our own lives requires that we use bodily appetites, passions, and powers in the way that leads to the highest fulfillment.

In this sense, therefore, as Nietzsche pointed out, chastity may be either just or unjust. It is possible for one to be continent and yet with "doggish lust to look out enviously on all that is done." The whole philosophy of the use of the body and material things is involved here.[6] In this connection it is enough to indicate that the

---

[6] See Chap. VII, "Lust and Gluttony into Timed Living" in *Conquering the Seven Deadly Sins.*

use of our sexual powers is not evil in itself, as many Christian ascetics and puritans have thought. These powers are meant to be used with joy and freedom in two ways: (1) as the accompaniment of spiritual love to enhance and beautify the relationship between husband and wife; and (2) for the reproduction of the race, in which husband and wife join together with the Divine Love in calling into being new persons. Therefore chastity, as a denial of these functions when their presence is right and needed, is gravely unjust.

Chastity is a virtue only as it is chosen by strong giving-love as the means to the good life for myself and others. It is a virtue when chosen as an act of sublimation in loving service to others, as in such persons as Florence Nightingale, Jane Addams, and Paul; or when practiced consciously as the alternative to indulging in extramarital or premarital experiences that could harm the marital relationships in my own home, present or future, or in the lives and homes of others. Chastity is a vice when used in an attempt to prove self-righteous superiority, because as such it produces merci-lessness and cruelty toward others and destroys the ability to live in harmony with my fellows.

Divorce

Consider, in its connection with the requirements of goodness and justice, the evils of a purely legalistic approach to the question of divorce. Should divorced persons ever be permitted to remarry? Suppose, says Archbishop William Temple, a man who is divorced by his first wife because of his infidelity marries again. This time he is faithful to his wife, who is a spiritually-minded woman through whose influence he begins to live a Christian life and to go to church. Should he be permitted to take the Communion with his children when they are confirmed? Some will say that these two people are living in sin, and that you cannot presume they are penitent until they are separated. "No," says the bishop, "I say that their separation at this stage would be merely another sin;

and it cannot be right to demand as the condition of restoration after a past sin that people should now sin against their new love and against their children." [7]

This is to say that what is important here is not a law but the welfare of this family! Two things must be considered in any question of right and wrong: the good principle which should be upheld and the highest good, present and future, for those involved.

Generally speaking, the good principle will not conflict with the highest good, but where it does, and obedience to the letter of the law is an enemy of the good of those involved, the law must always be subjugated to the requirements of love. God is not interested primarily in legal justice, in punishment for past mistakes, but in the present awareness and acceptance of his good will. True justice comes only when you are declared forgiven of past sins and begin to see and do what is the highest good in your *present circumstances*.

But it is equally true that the speedy and careless dissolution of the marriage bonds means injustice to both parties, and especially to the children. Hence the laws of divorce should be kept reasonably stringent in order that the warring couples may have time and opportunity to learn the way of harmony and love. Ideally man and woman are married into a divine union where they are to remain "until death us do part"!

Even when there is no union of real love, only a license from the state and perhaps a formal blessing by the church which permits a couple to live together without breaking the conventions of society, there is still hope. By patient growth, through struggles to new and deeper understanding and harmony, such an external union may become a true and spiritual one. This is what happens in a great many marriages. In all that are in any way successful, the degree of union is immeasurably heightened by the very struggles and disagreements through which they come as the years pass.

What is the husband or wife to do if the mate is disloyal, or

[7] *Centrality of Christ* (New York: Morehouse-Gorham Co., 1936), pp. 86-87.

attempts to subjugate the other by tyranny or cruelty, or deserts the other? Surely real giving-love will lead one to go the second or the tenth mile, to forgive seventy times seven, to do everything possible without the costliness of "peace at any price," to live peaceably with the other; but to say that there never comes a time when one should declare an end to a relationship that has been broken and misused, and has no apparent possibility of recovery, is to regard the well-being of a wife or husband and any children involved as less valuable than the keeping of a bargain. Such obedience to a law is unjust in the extreme.

To get a divorce may, under some circumstances, be the highest good for all concerned. It may cause the one who is offending to go into his or her crisis and discover that the self-centered way is destroying all that he really holds dear. Sometimes this may be the beginning of growing up. When it is, giving-love in the other party will always respond with encouragement and forgiveness. Or, the divorce may leave the offending party rejoicing over his so-called freedom to do as he pleases and becoming more and more walled-in by a shell of selfish neuroticism as he seeks to find others upon whom to vent his misery. Then the other has no choice but to build a life without the destructive influence of the sick one.

Many times both are in the wrong, both self-willed, stubborn, seeking their own way, and they are divorced before either begins to awaken and mature. Here again, the highest good, as in the case of the couple described by Archbishop Temple, might be to be married again to another person, this time to build on spiritual foundations and succeed. That such spiritual foundations will be built is far from certain. That they may be established and the second marriage become a genuine success is surely a real possibility and the only hope of divorcees who remarry. The folly of self-centered persons flitting from one marriage to another, attempting to find happiness, is pitiably obvious. No marriage can succeed apart from the willingness of both parties to grow up in generous, wise giving-love.

Marriage as an institution, like the Sabbath, was made for man and not man for the institution. The question of the right or wrong of divorce cannot be settled on the basis of a set of laws or rules, but only on the basis of the highest good for all involved, each case on its own merits. This is not to encourage divorce or to say that any two people who quarrel and fight have a right to call it quits. It is to say that giving-love will stick to the relationship as long as humanly possible. After the divorce seems to be necessary for the good of all concerned, giving-love still recognizes a responsibility toward the person whose obstinancy and sickness have prevented the marriage from succeeding. The offending one is still loved by God and therefore will be loved by the mature former husband or wife with the same kind of unmerited love that they give to any of God's children.

Temperance and Abstinence

Or consider the difference strong love makes in our approach to the evils of alcohol. It is good to encourage temperance and abstinence. In America the consumption of alcoholic beverages has increased by 100 per cent in the past fifteen years. This is tragic, especially in view of the fact that a large percentage of traffic accidents (variously estimated by police in different cities from 30 to 50 per cent) are directly or indirectly the result of it. If people did not drink there would never be an alcoholic, and there are from three to six million alcoholics suffering as only those who have been alcoholics know it is possible to suffer.

Of course, the problem of alcoholism is much more complex than the mere failure to abstain from the use of alcohol. The mental and emotional sickness that uses it as a means of escape from boredom, loneliness, or some other misery must be considered. However, it is still true that the suffering caused not only by alcoholism but often even by the moderate use of alcoholic beverage could not come except through alcohol. There are some who believe it can be used without doing an injustice to themselves or others; but even they will agree that its too frequent use is wrong and unjust. It is hard for others of us to see how its use at any time is ever truly just, considering the harmful possibilities.

However valuable the principle of temperance or abstinence, in practice it may become just another evidence of my superiority. Pointing the finger of scorn at "the sinful bum," we fall deeper into the sin of pride. "It is easy to learn to say, 'Except for the grace of God there am I.' It is very difficult really to feel the truth of it." [8] Temperance and abstinence are virtues only as they are the humble expression of my love for God, for myself, my family, my neighbor. They are vicious evils when used to raise myself, whether consciously or unconsciously, by lowering others.

Justice Without Love Is Unjust

There are countless illustrations of the hurt of self-righteous legalism. Let me cite only three.

There was the man who gave his life in a crusade against vice in general and all obscenity in particular. He was brave, heroic, and incorruptible; but at least fifteen people were driven to suicide by the exposure of their vice. His constant harping on a trivial vice made virtue itself seem priggish and unlovely and not a positive good. [9]

The second illustration is only one among hundreds that reveal the tragedy of self-righteousness as part of the cause of alcoholism. Roger L., one of 350 alcoholics interviewed by Howard J. Clinebell, Jr., described the lack of the love-that-never-fails in his home, thus: "My father was very stern. I was deathly afraid of him. . . . My mother was very much like my father—I never got much love from her. . . . She was a very righteous person, very moral." [10]

[8] Albion Roy King, in "Sin and Salvation," *Religion in Life* (Spring, 1952), p. 182.
[9] Dumas Malone, *Saints in Action* (New York: Abingdon Press, 1936), pp. 61-62.
[10] *Understanding and Counseling the Alcoholic* (Nashville: Abingdon Press, 1956), p. 47.

Alcohol became the means by which he tried to prove himself or exalt himself, and then to escape from himself. Both his father and mother were adamantly against alcohol and had taught him since childhood of its dangers, but neither had for him a strong, under-standing love that could have given him the security and freedom to be himself.[11] Obviously there were other causes for his alcohol-ism; the entire blame cannot be put on his parents. And yet some-where in his experience, as in that of almost every other alcoholic, there was the lack of the genuine love that could have given him the power of self-acceptance and prevented the false emotional compulsions which alcohol temporarily erased.

The same kind of self-righteousness in reverse causes some par-ents to be proud of their ability to "drink and to know when to stop." This causes them deliberately to encourage their children in the use of alcohol with its deadening, anesthetizing powers with-out regard to the fact that one or more of their children or friends may, through their influence, cross the line into compulsive drink-ing. Even the golden rule does not apply to persons who desire for themselves that which is hurtful and dangerous. In the case of alcohol, if I am to do unto others what I would have them do to me, the golden rule would mean presenting them with all the al-coholic beverages they could drink! Surely, on the other hand, strong love would say, "If my drinking causes my brother to stum-ble, I will not use alcoholic drink at all" (cf. I Cor. 8:13). Whether I choose the way of temperance or of total abstinence, my whole approach to the use of alcohol must be from the viewpoint of wise, strong love and not from self-righteousness.

The third illustration of the devastating injustice done by self-righteous justice is the story of the mother of a French countess who claimed to have a rigidly righteous and moral household but who was willing for her daughter to leave home or even to commit suicide rather than forgive her for her unconventional conduct. A

[11] See treatment in *Conquering the Seven Deadly Sins*, pp. 169 ff.

rigid justice was more important than mercy. Because of her disappointment in her father, due to his unfaithfulness to her mother, the daughter went out on a "fling" herself. According to her mother, she had brought shame and disgrace on the whole family. The mother was adamant—her daughter deserved to suffer complete isolation and abandonment. She said to the young priest who came trying to effect a reconciliation, "Some kinds of misunderstanding can never be bridged. One just gets used to them." The young priest answered, "Yes, madame, one gets used to not loving. Satan has profaned everything, even the resignation of saints. . . . What does family prestige matter to God, or dignity or culture, if it's all no more than a silk shroud on a rotting corpse." [12]

What more unholy profanation of virtue could there be than that which occurs over and over in so many of our homes where there is a rigid pattern of righteousness without giving-love! We may keep all the commandments, and yet not have enough strong, wise love in our hearts to be really concerned about others in such a way as to be able to help them. The lack of this love destroys the very virtue that we brag about. There is no real justice in the pursuit of self-righteousness.

Why Even the Law of Love Fails

Another kind of self-righteous justice is more difficult to recognize. Some of us reject the meticulous obedience to law and, instead, seize on Jesus' teaching about love. We decide to make love our final law. Jesus is our lawgiver in this respect, and his life our finest example. We determine that we will, by our own powers, develop a mature love in our own hearts, and thus be persons of integrity and rectitude in all our dealings.

We do not succeed for two serious reasons: First, because we do not have the wisdom to know what are the best gifts of love to others. We judge our acts by our own standards and find them good, and judge others by our own standards and find them so

---

[12] Bernanos, *op. cit.*, p. 159.

often evil. Our ideas of what is good are determined by our own experiences. Second, our unconscious minds are filled with fears and resentments from which in our own power we cannot escape.

We cannot force ourselves to love; hence our attempt to make obedience to the chief commandment, "Thou shalt love," the key of our lives is always to some degree a failure. Commanding selfish *me* to be unselfish, demanding that I who am filled with such bitterness and resentment shall have such feelings no longer is ordering myself to do the impossible.

"Don't be angry!" "Love your enemies." These and other admonitions are good counsel for anyone; determining to love by an act of the will is the first step toward loving. But if at the same time I am not drawing upon the resources of Eternal Love in which I find myself forgiven and accepted, my determination to love will be futile and unrealistic. For no one of us can root out his fears and resentments by an act of the will any more than he can stop the wind from blowing. Fears and resentments are symptoms of a deeper illness. Lacking self-acceptance in the loving security of God, I cannot overcome fear and hostility. A religion that relies on prideful self-will which at one moment decides to be loving and in the next is just as likely to give way to anger and hate is an unhealthy religion that in the long run produces more and more guilt, self-condemnation, and increasing mental illness. For if I think I have the power to conquer all resentments and fear by willing to do so without dealing with their basic cause, and then fail, I add a greater self-condemnation to my growing sense of guilt. I am truly unjust to myself.

Love with Justice—A Gift

"For God has done what the law, weakened by the flesh, could not do: sending his own Son . . ." The power to love we have been describing is a gift from God that comes to me through his act of self-giving love as evidenced in his Son and in those who have

163

caught his spirit—my mother or father, a friend, a minister, or some other great servant of mankind.

I cannot love by commanding myself to do so as a duty, for love is a gift. This is true of any part of life.

Any boy who plays football out of a sense of duty to his dad who wants him to be a star, or to his schoolmates who expect him to play, will not be a match for the heroes, including his dad whom he admires. His love for the game of football is *given* to him, and it is not something he can *create* in himself.

In the same way, a mother who cares for her baby entirely out of a sense of compulsion will not be able to give the baby the wise care which he needs to help him grow into emotional maturity. Why? Because she resents, perhaps unconsciously, the demands upon her time and energy which she desires to use elsewhere. Her hostilities will naturally be visited upon her baby, even though externally she does all she is supposed to do for him. The mother most likely to be a good mother is one who has received through others, and in her own times of prayer and worship, a strong sense of security in the love of God. She holds herself as loved and precious in the sight of the Eternal Mother-Father-God, and she passes this feeling of love and security on to her child.

Good deeds, however numerous, done out of a sense of duty or of obedience to good laws, can never remove from you the sense of guilt at your failure, your sense of inadequacy, your finiteness, your fears, your resentments. Nothing can do this except the sense of being related to the eternal, almighty God. "For God has done what the law, weakened by the flesh, could not do: sending his own Son . . ."

Only the forgiving, renewing love of God can ever make us just, and that not because of our works but through our faith. Justification by faith (Rom. 5:1) does not mean that our sins and failures in the past were really unimportant and therefore overlooked; but that in spite of them we are accepted and forgiven by God and given a peace and a hope that make it possible to act justly, courageously, wisely, in the present—or at least more so than in the past. I commit myself to act upon the conviction that I am thus accepted and forgiven.

Since we are justified by faith, we have peace with God through our Lord Jesus Christ. Through him we have obtained access to this grace in which we stand, and we rejoice in our hope of sharing the glory of God. More than that, we rejoice in our sufferings, knowing that suffering produces endurance, and endurance produces character, and character produces hope, and hope does not disappoint us, because God's love has been poured into our hearts through the Holy Spirit which has been given to us. (Rom. 5:1-5.)

Contained in these beautiful words of Paul is the basis of our greatest hope and joy. In this is our peace and our patience, our strength and our victory—the hope of sharing the glory of God. This glory of God in which we share is his wise and mighty agape love that is shed abroad in our hearts! Jesus' most revealing parable of this amazing love of the eternal Father is the parable of the prodigal son and his elder brother. (Luke 15:11-32.) When the father welcomed back the repentant son, the elder son was bitter:

Lo, these many years I have served you, and I never disobeyed your command [legally, righteously, I have done everything required by you]; yet you never gave me a kid, that I might make merry with my friends. [I deserved all you did for him and more, and yet you never did this for me.] But when this son of yours came . . .

Notice the painful lack of love in that last phrase.

Look at the answer Jesus says the father gave to this self-righteous elder son: "Son, you are always with me, and all that is mine is yours."

The elder brother, though outwardly obedient and virtuous, missed the greatest gift of all—the gift of his father's companionship and love; hence, he was unable to love his brother and therefore could not be just to him. The younger son, in all legalistic justice, deserved the suffering and a harsh reception instead of forgiveness; but he was accepted in the love of his father. Whatever future these two sons had, obviously only the younger could with his father possess the great virtue of strong love. Only he could attain to any measure of true justice.

Through the love of Christ and those who love with him, God is saying to us, "Son, you are always with me, and all that is mine is yours!"

Such amazing graciousness! Such immeasurable love! Such boundless security and freedom!

"What then shall we say to this? If God is for us, who is against us? . . . For I am sure that [nothing] will be able to separate us from the love of God in Christ Jesus our Lord!" (Rom. 8:31, 39.)

> My God, I love Thee, not because
> I hope for heaven thereby,
> Nor yet because, if I love not,
> I must forever die.
>
> .   .   .   .   .   .
>
> Not with the hope of gaining aught,
> Not seeking a reward,
> But as Thyself hast loved me,
> O ever-loving Lord;
> So would I love Thee, dearest Lord,
> And in Thy praise will sing,
> Because Thou art my loving God,
> And my eternal King.

Here is the never failing source of goodness that is always good and virtue that is forever virtuous. It is the strong, wise giving-love of God, in whom I live and move and have my being and through whom I find the power to love myself and others no matter the difficulty or the cost. In his Love I shall live, and my love, like his, shall never fail!

Love does conquer all!

A MEDITATION FOR THOSE
WHO WOULD BE JUST AND LOVING

Lord God of the Universe whom Jesus taught me to call Father, in whom justice and mercy meet, whose righteousness does not prevent thy mercy and whose mercy does not cancel thy justice;

I need thy forgiveness, not only for my conscious sins, but for my virtues that have been used to prop up my sagging house of life and to give me the false assurance that I am good and just.

With amazement and love, I accept thy forgiveness! I do not deserve it but thou hast declared me deserving and just, because I am thy son, the recipient of thy loving care.

I too have wandered into a far country, where I have lost and wasted my finest powers and have tried to satisfy my soul on the husks of egoistic pleasure and achievement.

Unsatisfied and hollow still, my soul is empty of real joy and peace. I have tried to fill this hollowness with mere artificial things that leave me still empty and bereft.

O Father, in thy presence is fullness of joy. In thy house there is plenty and to spare; and here in my self-made wilderness there is only poverty and frustration.

This moment, by faith and trust, I arise and enter into thy house of life in which there is joy forever. In thy loving presence I find myself and my brother, loved and made whole.

It is too much for me! I cannot understand it; but I receive it with awe and a joyous determination to act worthily, to do justly, to love mercy, and to walk humbly before the Lord.

Rejoice, give thanks, and sing!

God's Love Conquers All!

167

INDEX

169

171

173

174